AMERICA

AMERICA

*Classics That Help Define
the Nation*

THE MODERN LIBRARY

NEW YORK

1999 Modern Library Edition

Compilation copyright © 1999 by Random House, Inc.

LIBRARY OF CONGRESS CATALOGING-IN-PUBLICATION DATA
America: classics that help define the nation.—1999 Modern Library ed.
p.   cm.
ISBN 0-375-75381-8
1. National characteristics, American—Literary collections.
2. United States—Civilization—Literary collections.   3. United States—
Civilization—Sources.   4. American literature.   I. Modern Library (Firm)
PS509.U52A36   1999
810.8'0358—dc21   99-11787

Modern Library website address: www.modernlibrary.com

Printed in the United States of America on acid-free paper

2   4   6   8   9   7   5   3   1

PREFACE

This book is the fifth in the series of Modern Library collections of stories and verse, following *Christmas Classics, Mothers, The Raven and the Monkey's Paw* (a Halloween book concentrating on the works of Edgar Allan Poe), and *Love*. The subject matter of these first four books is clear, and they all could run to more than one volume: There are many Christmas stories; more that concern our mothers; somewhat fewer about ghosts and the supernatural; but an almost bottomless well of literature that deals with love, however it is defined. *America*, though, is a little more difficult to describe. It draws from nothing less than a nation and its history, as recorded in words.

The Florentine navigator Amerigo Vespucci (1454–1512) lent his name to the continent the coastline of which his expeditions explored around the beginning of the sixteenth century. Actually, his longest voyage was to what is now recognized as South America. Of course, there were already settled, advanced civilizations there. As the expeditions got larger and European settlement increased, these existing populations were displaced. As Daniel Boorstin has written, "A new civilization was being born less out of plans and purposes than out of the unsettlement which the New World brought to the ways of the Old." Eventually, Europeans colonized the Americas and new countries were created. Now, colloquially, when someone says "America," they usually mean the United States. This is how the editors of this book have used the word and concentrated their attention. They have collected some of the writings that have helped to define this nation and to distinguish what Vespucci meant by "America" from what constitutes the United States today.

Now the country is mature, somewhere in its adulthood. It is a stage at which a person's character is fully defined. If a nation can have a character, it grows out of its people and the accumulation of the changes they effect over time. The study of history helps to identify what has come to define it. One vital element is how the people of a country decide to govern themselves, and another is their art. *America* is able to take a few examples from each. More has been left out than can even be alluded to in these pages. Some is by necessity. There is no visual art and no music, the latter a particular fault when so much of the nation's heritage is captured in song and when jazz might be the quintessential American art form. The selections tend toward the nineteenth century, when the country expanded to its present size and matured. It neglects the present. But what is contained within these pages might help to describe July Fourth and the flag and all that they have come to represent. It can only hope to resemble some people's America.

*   *   *

The first selection is *The Mayflower Compact*, a document drawn up by the settlers now known as the Pilgrim Fathers on board the *Mayflower*, the ship that brought them from the Old World to the New. As they approached the coastline of what would become New England, they agreed to work together in the manner described. As the historian William Bradford wrote, there were already jurisdictional conflicts concerning the new lands, and the *Mayflower* voyagers were keen to establish a covenant before they reached land.

CONTENTS

THE SOUTH

THE WEST

THE GREAT CITIES

AMERICANS

FIVE SPEECHES

ANTHEMS AND SONGS

AMERICA

THE MAYFLOWER COMPACT

In the name of God Amen. We whose names are underwriten, the loyall subjects of our dread soveraigne Lord King James by the grace of God, of great Britaine, Franc, & Ireland king, defender of the faith, &c.

Haveing undertaken, for the glorie of God, and advancements of the Christian faith and honour of our king & countrie, a voyage to plant the first colonie in the Northerne parts of Virginia, doe by these presents solemnly & mutualy in the presence of God, and one of another, covenant & combine our selves togeather into a civill body politick; for our better ordering, & preservation & furtherance of the ends aforesaid; and by vertue hearof to enacte, constitute, and frame shuch just & equall lawes, ordinances, Acts, constitutions, & offices, from time to time, as shall be thought most meete & convenient for the generall good of the Colonie: unto which we promise all due submission and obedience.

In witnes whereof we have hereunder subscribed our names at Cap-Codd the • 11 • of November, in the year the raigne of our soveraigne Lord King James of England, France, & Ireland the eighteenth and of Scotland the fiftie fourth. An°: Dom. 1620.

John Carver
William Bradford
Edward Winslow
William Brewster
Isaac Allerton
Myles Standish
John Alden
Samuel Fuller
Christopher Martin
William Mullins
William White
Richard Warren
John Howland
Stephen Hopkins
Edward Tilley
John Tilley
Francis Cooke
Thomas Rogers
John Turner
Francis Eaton
James Chilton
John Crakston
John Billington
Moses Fletcher
John Goodman
Degory Priest
Thomas Williams
Gilbert Winslow
Edmund Margeson
Peter Brown
Richard Britterige
George Soule
Richard Clarke
Richard Gardiner
John Allerton
Thomas English
Thomas Tinker

John Rigdale
Edward Fuller
Edward Doty
Edward Leister

THE
REVOLUTIONARIES

In 1861, Henry Wadsworth Longfellow (1807–1882) published his poem that celebrates the legendary midnight ride of Paul Revere in which an innkeeper describes the heroic efforts of the rider who warns of the British invasion. Three other pieces describe some of the main actors of the war of independence. Philip Freneau (1752–1832) was "the Poet of the American Revolution" and was himself imprisoned during the war by the British. His poem eulogizes the statesman Benjamin Franklin (1706–1790), who, among myriad achievements, helped to draft the Declaration of Independence and was instrumental in the adoption of the American Constitution. The character of the first president, George Washington (1732–1799), is described first by the Romantic poet Lord Byron (1788–1824) and then, less effusively and in prose, by Thomas Jefferson (1743–1826), the third president.

PAUL REVERE'S RIDE

Henry Wadsworth Longfellow

Listen, my children, and you shall hear
Of the midnight ride of Paul Revere,
On the eighteenth of April, in Seventy-five;
Hardly a man is now alive
Who remembers that famous day and
     year.

He said to his friend, "If the British march
By land or sea from the town to-night,
Hang a lantern aloft in the belfry arch
Of the North Church tower as a signal
     light,—
One, if by land, and two, if by sea;
And I on the opposite shore will be,
Ready to ride and spread the alarm
Through every Middlesex village and farm,
For the country folk to be up and to arm."

Then he said, "Good night!" and with muffled
     oar
Silently rowed to the Charlestown shore,
Just as the moon rose over the bay,
Where swinging wide at her moorings lay
The Somerset, British man-of-war;
A phantom ship, with each mast and spar
Across the moon like a prison bar,
And a huge black hulk, that was magnified
By its own reflection in the tide.

Meanwhile, his friend, through alley and street,
Wanders and watches with eager ears,
Till in the silence around him he hears

The muster of men at the barrack door,
The sound of arms, and the tramp of feet,
And the measured tread of the grenadiers,
Marching down to their boats on the shore.

Then he climbed the tower of the Old North
        Church,
By the wooden stairs, with stealthy tread,
To the belfry-chamber overhead,
And startled the pigeons from their perch
On the sombre rafters, that round him made
Masses and moving shapes of shade,—
By the trembling ladder, steep and tall,
To the highest window in the wall,
Where he paused to listen and look down
A moment on the roofs of the town,
And the moonlight flowing over all.

Beneath, in the churchyard, lay the dead,
In their night-encampment on the hill,
Wrapped in silence so deep and still
That he could hear, like a sentinel's tread,
The watchful night-wind, as it went
Creeping along from tent to tent,
And seeming to whisper, "All is well!"
A moment only he feels the spell
Of the place and the hour, and the secret dread
Of the lonely belfry and the dead;
For suddenly all his thoughts are bent
On a shadowy something far away,
Where the river widens to meet the bay,—
A line of black that bends and floats
On the rising tide, like a bridge of boats.

Meanwhile, impatient to mount and ride,
Booted and spurred, with a heavy stride
On the opposite shore walked Paul Revere.

Now he patted his horse's side,
Now gazed at the landscape far and near,
Then, impetuous, stamped the earth,
And turned and tightened his saddle-girth;
But mostly he watched with eager search
The belfry-tower of the Old North Church,
As it rose above the graves on the hill,
Lonely and spectral and sombre and still.
And lo! as he looks, on the belfry's height
A glimmer, and then a gleam of light!
He springs to the saddle, the bridle he turns,
But lingers and gazes, till full on his sight
A second lamp in the belfry burns!

A hurry of hoofs in a village street,
A shape in the moonlight, a bulk in the dark,
And beneath, from the pebbles, in passing, a spark
Struck out by a steed flying fearless and fleet:
That was all! And yet, through the gloom and the light,
The fate of a nation was riding that night;
And the spark struck out by that steed, in his flight,
Kindled the land into flame with its heat.

He has left the village and mounted the steep,
And beneath him, tranquil and broad and deep,
Is the Mystic, meeting the ocean tides;
And under the alders that skirt its edge,
Now soft on the sand, now loud on the ledge,
Is heard the tramp of his steed as he rides.

It was twelve by the village clock,
When he crossed the bridge into Medford town.
He heard the crowing of the cock,
And the barking of the farmer's dog,
And felt the damp of the river fog,
That rises after the sun goes down.

It was one by the village clock,
When he galloped into Lexington.
He saw the gilded weathercock
Swim in the moonlight as he passed,
And the meeting-house windows, blank and
    bare,
Gaze at him with a spectral glare,
As if they already stood aghast
At the bloody work they would look upon.

It was two by the village clock,
When he came to the bridge in Concord town.
He heard the bleating of the flock,
And the twitter of birds among the trees,
And felt the breath of the morning breeze
Blowing over the meadows brown.
And one was safe and asleep in his bed
Who at the bridge would be first to fall,
Who that day would be lying dead,
Pierced by a British musket-ball.

You know the rest. In the books you have read,
How the British Regulars fired and fled,—
How the farmers gave them ball for ball,
From behind each fence and farm-yard wall,
Chasing the red-coats down the lane,
Then crossing the fields to emerge again
Under the trees at the turn of the road,
And only pausing to fire and load.

So through the night rode Paul Revere;
And so through the night went his cry of alarm
To every Middlesex village and farm,—
A cry of defiance and not of fear,
A voice in the darkness, a knock at the door,
And a word that shall echo forevermore!
For, borne on the night-wind of the Past,

Through all our history, to the last,
In the hour of darkness and peril and need,
The people will waken and listen to hear
The hurrying hoof-beats of that steed,
And the midnight message of Paul Revere.

On the Death of Benjamin Franklin

Philip Freneau

Thus, some tall tree that long hath stood
The glory of its native wood,
By storms destroyed, or length of years,
Demands the tribute of our tears.

The pile, that took long time to raise,
To dust returns by slow decays;
But, when its destined years are o'er,
We must regret the loss the more.

So long accustomed to your aid,
The world laments your exit made;
So long befriended by your art,
Philosopher, 't is hard to part!—

When monarchs tumble to the ground
Successors easily are found;
But, matchless Franklin! what a few
Can hope to rival such as you,
Who seized from kings their sceptred pride,
And turned the lightning's darts aside!

WASHINGTON

Lord Byron

Where may the wearied eye repose
When gazing on the Great;
Where neither guilty glory glows,
Nor despicable state?
Yes—one—the first—the last—the best—
The Cincinnatus of the West,
Whom envy dared not hate,
Bequeath the name of Washington,
To make men blush there was but one!

THE CHARACTER OF
GEORGE WASHINGTON

Thomas Jefferson

. . . . I think I knew General Washington intimately and thoroughly; and were I called on to delineate his character, it should be in terms like these.

His mind was great and powerful, without being of the very first order; his penetration strong, though not so acute as that of a Newton, Bacon, or Locke; and as far as he saw, no judgment was ever sounder. It was slow in operation, being little aided by invention or imagination, but sure in conclusion. Hence the common remark of his officers, of the advantage he derived from councils of war, where hearing all suggestions, he selected whatever was best; and certainly no general ever planned his battles more judiciously. But if deranged during the course of the action, if any member of his plan was dislocated by sudden circumstances, he was slow in re-adjustment. The consequence was, that he often failed in the field, and rarely against an enemy in station, as at Boston and York. He was incapable of fear, meeting personal dangers with the calmest unconcern. Perhaps the strongest feature in his character was prudence, never acting until every circumstance, every consideration, was maturely weighed; refraining if he saw a doubt, but, when once decided, going through with his purpose, whatever obstacles opposed. His integrity was most pure, his justice the most inflexible I have ever known, no motives of interest or consanguinity, of friendship or hatred, being able to bias his decision. He was, indeed, in every sense of the words, a wise, a good, and a great man. His temper was naturally irritable and high toned; but reflection and resolution had obtained a firm and habitual ascendency over it. If ever, however, it broke its bonds, he was most tremendous in his wrath. In his expenses he was honorable, but exact; liberal in contributions to whatever promised utility; but frowning and unyielding on all visionary projects, and all unworthy calls on his charity. His heart was not warm in its affections; but he exactly calculated every man's value, and gave him a solid esteem proportioned to it. His person, you know, was fine, his stature exactly what one would wish, his deportment easy, erect and noble; the best horseman of his age, and the most graceful figure that could be seen on horseback. Although in the circle of his friends, where he might be unreserved with safety, he took a free share in conversation, his colloquial talents were not above mediocrity, possessing neither copiousness of ideas, nor fluency of words. In public, when called on for a sudden opinion, he was unready, short and embarrassed. Yet he wrote readily, rather diffusely, in an easy and correct style. This he had acquired by conversation with the world, for his education was merely reading, writing and common arithmetic, to which he added surveying at a later day. His time was employed in action chiefly, reading little, and that only in agriculture and English history. His correspondence became necessarily extensive, and, with journalizing his agricultural proceedings, occupied most of his leisure hours within doors. On the whole, his character was, in its mass, perfect, in nothing bad, in few points indifferent; and it may truly be said, that never did nature and fortune combine more perfectly to make a man great, and to place him in the same constellation with whatever worthies have merited from man an everlasting remembrance. For his was the singular destiny and merit, of leading the armies of his country successfully through an arduous war, for the establishment of its independence; of conducting its councils through the birth of a government, new in its forms and principles, until it had settled down into a quiet and orderly train; and of scrupulously obeying the laws through the whole of his career, civil and military, of which the history of the world furnishes no other example.

. . . . I am satisfied the great body of republicans think of him as I do.

We were, indeed, dissatisfied with him on his ratification of the British treaty. But this was short lived. We knew his honesty, the wiles with which he was encompassed, and that age had already begun to relax the firmness of his purposes; and I am convinced he is more deeply seated in the love and gratitude of the republicans, than in the Pharisaical homage of the federal monarchists. For he was no monarchist from preference of his judgment. The soundness of that gave him correct views of the rights of man, and his severe justice devoted him to them. He has often declared to me that he considered our new Constitution as an experiment on the practicability of republican government, and with what dose of liberty man could be trusted for his own good; that he was determined the experiment should have a fair trial, and would lose the last drop of his blood in support of it. And these declarations he repeated to me the oftener and more pointedly, because he knew my suspicions of Colonel Hamilton's views, and probably had heard from him the same declarations which I had, to wit, "that the British constitution, with its unequal representation, corruption and other existing abuses, was the most perfect government which had ever been established on earth, and that a reformation of those abuses would make it an impracticable government." I do believe that General Washington had not a firm confidence in the durability of our government. He was naturally distrustful of men, and inclined to gloomy apprehensions; and I was ever persuaded that a belief that we must at length end in something like a British constitution, had some weight in his adoption of the ceremonies of levees, birthdays, pompous meetings with Congress, and other forms of the same character, calculated to prepare us gradually for a change which he believed possible, and to let it come on with as little shock as might be to the public mind.

These are my opinions of General Washington, which I would vouch at the judgment seat of God, having been formed on an acquaintance of thirty years. I served with him in the Virginia legislature from 1769 to the Revolutionary war, and again, a short time in Congress, until he left us to take command of the army. During the war and after it we corresponded occasionally, and in the four years of my continuance in the office of Secretary of State, our intercourse was daily, confidential and cordial. After I retired from that office, great and malignant pains were taken by our federal monarchists, and not entirely without effect, to make him view me as a theorist, holding French principles of government, which would lead infallibly to licentiousness and anarchy. And to this he listened the more easily, from my known disapprobation of the British treaty. I never saw him afterwards, or these malignant insinuations should have been dissipated before his just judgment, as mists before the sun. I felt on his death, with my countrymen, that "verily a great man hath fallen this day in Israel."

EXPLORATION

After independence, the new Americans steadily expanded the jurisdiction of the country westward. The first great expedition that explored the new land was undertaken by Captains Meriwether Lewis and William Clark, who, between 1804 and 1806, traveled more than eight thousand miles between the Missouri River and the Pacific. Lewis (1774–1809) worked as President Jefferson's private secretary before the journey and was governor of the Louisiana Territory from 1807 until his mysterious and untimely death. Clark (1770–1838), a fellow Virginian, went on to serve as governor of the Missouri Territory. Their descriptions of lands and animals never seen before by Europeans contrast with the experience of the historian Francis Parkman (1823–1893), who found a busy frontier west of St. Louis in 1846 as he set off to write a history of the struggle between the English and the French for domination of the continent. Twenty years before Theodore Roosevelt became the twenty-sixth president in 1904, and following the death of his wife, Alice, in childbirth, he left New York for a ranch in the Dakota Badlands. He chronicled the American interior in a number of books, including The Wilderness Hunter *(1893), which includes this account of the emergence and passing of the hunter in the American heartland. The poet Edwin Arlington Robinson (1869–1935) describes the Klondike—a tributary of the Yukon River in western Canada where gold was found in 1896. Tens of thousands of prospectors flooded the area in search of "the golden river." The readily available deposits were soon exhausted, but commercial mining was not suspended until 1969.*

FROM

The Journals of Lewis and Clark

Thursday May 9th. 1805

Capt C. killed 2 bucks and 2 buffaloe, I also killed one buffaloe which
proved to be the best meat, it was in tolerable order; we saved the best of
the meat, and from the cow I killed we saved the necessary materials for
making what our wrighthand cook Charbono calls the *boudin* (*poudingue*)
blanc, and immediately set him about preparing them for supper; this
white pudding we all esteem one of the greatest del[ic]acies of the for-
rest, it may not be amiss therefore to give it a place. About 6 feet of the
lower extremity of the large gut of the Buffaloe is the first mo[r]sel that
the cook makes love to, this he holds fast at one end with the right hand,
while the forefinger and thumb of the left he gently compresses it, and
discharges what he says *is not good to eat,* but of which in the sequel we get
a moderate portion; the mustle lying underneath the shoulder blade
next to the back, and fillets are next saught, these are needed up very fine
with a good portion of kidney suet; to this composition is then added a
just proportion of pepper and salt and a small quantity of flour; thus far
advanced, our skilfull opporator Charbono seizes his recepticle, which
has never once touched the water, for that would intirely distroy the
regular order of the whole procedure; you will not forget that the side
you now see is that covered with a good coat of fat provided the animal

be in good order; the operator sceizes the recepticle I say, and tying it fast at one end turns it inward and begins now with repeated evolutions of the hand and arm, and a brisk motion of the finger and thumb to put in what he says is *bon pour manger;* thus by stuffing and compressing he soon distends the recepticle to the utmost limmits of it's power of expansion, and in the course of it's longtudinal progress it drives from the other end of the recepticle a much larger portion of the [?] than was previously discharged by the finger and thumb of the left hand in a former part of the operation; thus when the sides of the recepticle are skilfully exchanged the outer for the iner, and all is compleately filled with something good to eat, it is tyed at the other end, but not any cut off, for that would make the pattern too scant; it is then baptised in the missouri with two dips and a flirt, and bobbed into the kettle; from whence, after it be well boiled it is taken and fryed with bears oil untill it becomes brown, when it is ready to esswage the pangs of a keen appetite or such as travelers in the wilderness are seldom at a loss for.

We saw a great quantity of game today particularly of Elk and Buffaloe, the latter are now so gentle that the men frequently throw sticks and stones at them in order to drive them out of the way. We also saw this evening emence quantities of timber cut by the beaver which appeared to have been done the preceeding year, in one place particularly they had cut all the timber down for three acres in front and on nearly one back from the river and had removed a considerable proportion of it, the timber grew very thick and some of it was as large as a man's body. The river for several days has been as wide as it is generally near it's mouth, tho' it is much shallower or I should begin to dispair of ever reaching it's source; it has been crouded today with many sandbars; the water also appears to become clearer, it has changed it's complexin very considerably. I begin to feel extreemly anxious to get in view of the rocky mountains.

I killed four plover this evening of a different species from any I have yet seen; it resembles the grey or whistling plover more than any other of this family of birds; it is about the size of the yellow legged or large grey plover common to the lower part of this river as well as most parts of the Atlantic States where they are sometimes called the Jack curloo; the eye is moderately large, are black with a narrow ring of dark yellowish brown; the head, neck, upper part of the body and coverts of the wings are of a dove coloured brown, which when the bird is at rest is the predominant colour; the brest and belley are of a brownish white; the tail is composed of 12 feathers of 3 Ins. being of equal length, of these the two in the center are black, with traverse bars of yellowish brown; the others are a brownish white. The large feathers of the wings are white tiped with blacked. The beak is black, 2½ inches in length, slightly tapering, streight, of a cilindric form and blontly or roundly pointed; the chaps are of equal length, and nostrils narrow longitudional and connected; the feet and legs are smoth and of a greenish brown; has three long toes and a short one on each foot, the long toes are unconnected with a web, and the short one is placed very high up the leg behind, insomuch that it dose not touch the ground when the bird stands erect. The notes of this bird are louder and more various than any other of this family that I have seen.

FROM

THE OREGON TRAIL

Francis Parkman

THE FRONTIER

Last spring, 1846, was a busy season in the city of St. Louis. Not only were emigrants from every part of the country preparing for the journey to Oregon and California, but an unusual number of traders were making ready their wagons and outfits for Santa Fé. The hotels were crowded, and the gunsmiths and saddlers were kept constantly at work in providing arms and equipments for the different parties of travellers. Steamboats were leaving the levee and passing up the Missouri, crowded with passengers on their way to the frontier.

In one of these, the "Radnor," since snagged and lost, my friend and relative Quincy Adams Shaw, and myself left St. Louis on the 28th of April, on a tour of curiosity and amusement to the Rocky Mountains. The boat was loaded until the water broke alternately over her guards. Her upper-deck was covered with large wagons of a peculiar form, for the Santa Fé trade, and her hold was crammed with goods for the same destination. There were also the equipments and provisions of a party of Oregon emigrants, a band of mules and horses, piles of saddles and harness, and a multitude of nondescript articles, indispensable on the prairies. Almost hidden in this medley was a small French cart, of the sort very appropriately called a "mule-killer" beyond the frontiers, and not far distant a tent, together with a miscellaneous assortment of boxes and barrels. The whole equipage was far from prepossessing in its appearance; yet, such as it was, it was destined to a long and arduous journey, on which the persevering reader will accompany it.

The passengers on board the "Radnor" corresponded with her freight. In her cabin were Santa Fé traders, gamblers, speculators, and adventurers of various descriptions, and her steerage was crowded with Oregon emigrants, "mountain men," negroes, and a party of Kanzas Indians, who had been on a visit to St. Louis.

Thus laden the boat struggled upward for seven or eight days against the rapid current of the Missouri, grating upon snags, and hanging for two or three hours at a time upon sand-bars. We entered the mouth of the Missouri in a drizzling rain, but the weather soon became clear, and showed distinctly the broad and turbid river, with its eddies, its sand-bars, its ragged islands, and forest-covered shores. The Missouri is constantly changing its course,—wearing away its banks on one side, while it forms new ones on the other. Its channel is continually shifting. Islands are formed, and then washed away; and while the old forests on one side are undermined and swept off, a young growth springs up from the new soil upon the other. With all these changes the water is so charged with mud and sand that, in spring, it is perfectly opaque, and in a few minutes deposits a sediment an inch thick in the bottom of a tumbler. The river was now high; but when we descended in the autumn it was fallen very low, and all the secrets of its treacherous shallows were exposed to view. It was frightful to see the dead and broken trees, thick-set as a military abattis, firmly imbedded in the sand, and all pointing down stream, ready to impale any unhappy steamboat that at high water should pass over them.

In five or six days we began to see signs of the great western movement that was taking place. Parties of emigrants, with their tents and wagons, were encamped on open spots near the bank, on their way to the common rendezvous at Independence. On a rainy day, near sunset, we reached the landing of this place, which is some miles from the river, on the extreme frontier of Missouri. The scene was characteristic, for here were represented at one view the most remarkable features of this wild and enterprising region. On the muddy shore stood some thirty or forty dark, slavish-looking Spaniards, gazing stupidly out from beneath their broad hats. They were attached to one of the Santa Fé companies, whose wagons were crowded together on the banks above. In the midst of these, crouching over a smouldering fire, was a group of Indians, belonging to a remote Mexican tribe. One or two French hunters from the mountains, with their long hair and buckskin dresses, were looking at the boat; and seated on a log close at hand were three men, with rifles lying across their knees. The foremost of these, a tall, strong figure, with a clear blue eye and an open, intelligent face, might very well represent that race of restless and intrepid pioneers whose axes and rifles have opened a path from the Alleghanies to the western prairies. He was on his way to Oregon, probably a more congenial field to him than any that now remained on this side of the great plains.

Early on the next morning we reached Kanzas, about five hundred miles from the mouth of the Missouri. Here we landed, and leaving our equipments in charge of Colonel Chick, whose log-house was the substitute for a tavern, we set out in a wagon for Westport, where we hoped to procure mules and horses for the journey.

It was a remarkably fresh and beautiful May morning. The woods, through which the miserable road conducted us, were lighted by the bright sunshine and enlivened by a multitude of birds. We overtook on the way our late fellow-travellers, the Kanzas Indians, who adorned with all their finery were proceeding homeward at a round pace; and whatever they might have seemed on board the boat, they made a very striking and picturesque feature in the forest landscape.

Westport was full of Indians, whose little shaggy ponies were tied by dozens along the houses and fences. Sacs and Foxes, with shaved heads and painted faces, Shawanoes and Delawares, fluttering in calico frocks and turbans, Wyandots dressed like white men, and a few wretched Kanzas wrapped in old blankets, were strolling about the streets or lounging in and out of the shops and houses.

As I stood at the door of the tavern I saw a remarkable-looking personage coming up the street. He had a ruddy face, garnished with the stumps of a bristly red beard and moustache; on one side of his head was a round cap with a knob at the top, such as Scottish laborers sometimes wear; his coat was of a nondescript form, and made of a gray Scotch plaid, with the fringes hanging all about it; he wore trousers of coarse homespun, and hobnailed shoes; and to complete his equipment, a little black pipe was stuck in one corner of his mouth. In this curious attire, I recognized Captain C——, of the British army, who, with his brother, and Mr. R——, an English gentleman, was bound on a hunting expedition across the continent. I had seen the Captain and his companions at St. Louis. They had now been for some time at Westport, making preparations for their departure, and waiting for a reinforcement, since they were too few in number to attempt it alone. They might, it is true, have joined some of the parties of emigrants who were on the point of setting out for Oregon and California; but they professed great disinclination to have any connection with the "Kentucky fellows."

The Captain now urged it upon us that we should join forces and proceed to the mountains in company. Feeling no greater partiality for the society of the emigrants than they did, we thought the arrangement a good one, and consented to it. Our future fellow-travellers had installed themselves in a little log-house, where we found them surrounded by saddles, harness, guns, pistols, telescopes, knives, and in short their complete appointments for the prairie. R——, who had a taste for natural history, sat at a table stuffing a woodpecker; the brother of the Captain, who was an Irishman, was splicing a trail-rope on the floor. The Captain pointed out, with much complacency, the different articles of their outfit. "You see," said he, "that we are all old travellers. I am convinced that no party ever went upon the prairie better provided." The hunter whom they had employed, a surly-looking Canadian, named Sorel, and their muleteer, an American ruffian from St. Louis, were lounging about the building. In a little log stable close at hand were their horses and mules, selected with excellent judgment by the Captain.

We left them to complete their arrangements, while we pushed our own to all convenient speed. The emigrants, for whom our friends professed such contempt were encamped on the prairie about eight or ten miles distant, to the number of a thousand or more, and new parties were constantly passing out from Independence to join them. They were in great confusion, holding meetings, passing resolutions, and drawing up regulations, but unable to unite in the choice of leaders to conduct them across the prairie. Being at leisure one day, I rode over to Independence. The town was crowded. A multitude of shops had sprung up to furnish the emigrants and Santa Fé traders with necessaries for their journey; and there was an incessant hammering and banging from a dozen blacksmiths' sheds, where the heavy wagons were being repaired, and the horses and oxen shod. The streets were thronged with men, horses, and mules. While I was in the town, a train of emigrant wagons from Illinois passed through, to join the camp on the prairie, and stopped in the principal street. A multitude of healthy children's faces were peeping out from under the covers of the wagons. Here and there a buxom damsel was seated on horseback, holding over her sunburnt face an old umbrella or a parasol, once gaudy enough, but now miserably faded. The men, very sober-looking countrymen, stood about their oxen; and as I passed I noticed three old fellows, who, with their long whips in their hands, were zealously discussing the doctrine of regeneration. The emigrants, however, are not all of this stamp. Among them are some of the vilest outcasts in the country. I have often perplexed myself to divine the various motives that give impulse to this migration; but whatever they may be, whether an insane hope of a better condition in life, or a desire of shaking off restraints of law and society, or mere restlessness, certain it is that multitudes bitterly repent the journey, and, after they have reached the land of promise, are happy enough to escape from it.

In the course of seven or eight days we had brought our preparations nearly to a close. Meanwhile our friends had completed theirs, and, becoming tired of Westport, they told us that they would set out in advance, and wait at the crossing of the Kanzas till we should come up. Accordingly R——and the muleteer went forward with the wagon and tent, while the Captain and his brother, together with Sorel and a trapper named Boisverd, who had joined them, followed with the band of horses. The commencement of the journey was ominous, for the captain was scarcely a mile from Westport, riding along in state at the head of his party, leading his intended buffalo horse by a rope, when a tremendous thunder-storm came on and drenched them all to the skin. They hurried on to reach the place, about seven miles off, where R——was to have had the camp in readiness to receive them. But this prudent person, when he saw the storm approaching, had selected a sheltered glade in the woods, where he pitched his tent, and was sipping a comfortable cup of coffee while the Captain galloped for miles beyond through the rain to look for him. At length the storm cleared away, and the sharp-eyed trapper succeeded in discovering his tent. R——had by this time finished his coffee, and was seated on a buffalo-robe smoking his pipe. The Captain was one of the most easy-tempered men in existence, so he bore his ill-luck with great composure, shared the dregs of the coffee with his brother, and lay down to sleep in his wet clothes.

We ourselves had our share of the deluge. We were leading a pair of mules to Kanzas when the storm broke. Such sharp and incessant flashes of lightning, such stunning and continuous thunder I had never known before. The woods were completely obscured by the diagonal sheets of rain that fell with a heavy roar, and rose in spray from the ground, and the streams swelled so rapidly that we could hardly ford them. At length, looming through the rain, we saw the log-house of Colonel Chick, who received us with his usual bland hospitality; while his wife, who, though a little soured and stiffened by a long course of camp-meetings, was not behind him in good-will, supplied us with the means of bettering our drenched and bedraggled condition. The storm clearing away at about sunset opened a noble prospect from the porch of the Colonel's house which stands upon a high hill. The sun streamed from the breaking clouds upon the swift and angry Missouri, and on the vast expanse of forest that stretched from its banks back to the distant bluffs.

Returning on the next day to Westport we received a message from the Captain, who had ridden back to deliver it in person, but finding that we were in Kanzas, had intrusted it to an acquaintance of his, named Vogel, who kept a small grocery and liquor shop. Whiskey, by the way, circulates more freely in Westport than is altogether safe in a place where every man carries a loaded pistol in his pocket. As we passed this establishment we saw Vogel's broad German face thrust from his door. He said he had something to tell us, and invited us to take a dram. Neither his liquor nor his message was very palatable. The Captain had returned to give us notice that R——, who assumed the direction of his party had determined upon another route from that agreed upon between us; and instead of taking the course of the traders, had resolved to pass northward by Fort Leavenworth, and follow the path marked out by the dragoons in their expedition of last summer. To adopt such a plan without consulting us, we looked upon as a high-handed proceeding; but suppressing our dissatisfaction as well as we could, we made up our minds to join them at Fort Leavenworth, where they were to wait for us.

Accordingly, our preparation being now complete, we attempted one fine morning to begin our journey. The first step was an unfortunate one. No sooner were our animals put in harness than the shaft-mule reared and plunged, burst ropes and straps, and nearly flung the cart into the Missouri. Finding her wholly uncontrollable, we exchanged her for another, with which we were furnished by our friend Mr. Boone, of Westport, a grandson of Daniel Boone, the pioneer. This foretaste of prairie experience was very soon followed by another. Westport was scarcely out of sight when we encountered a deep muddy gully, of a species that afterward became but too familiar to us, and here for the space of an hour or more the cart stuck fast.

FROM

THE WILDERNESS HUNTER

Theodore Roosevelt

THE AMERICAN WILDERNESS

Manifold are the shapes taken by the American wilderness. In the east, from the Atlantic coast to the Mississippi valley, lies a land of magnificent hardwood forest. In endless variety and beauty, the trees cover the ground, save only where they have been cleared away by man, or where towards the west the expanse of the forest is broken by fertile prairies. Towards the north, this region of hardwood trees merges insensibly into the southern extension of the great subarctic forest; here the silver stems of birches gleam against the sombre background of coniferous evergreens. In the southeast again, by the hot, oozy coasts of the South Atlantic and the Gulf, the forest becomes semi-tropical; palms wave their feathery fronds, and the tepid swamps teem with reptile life.

Some distance beyond the Mississippi, stretching from Texas to North Dakota, and westward to the Rocky Mountains, lies the plains country. This is a region of light rainfall, where the ground is clad with short grass, while cottonwood trees fringe the courses of the winding plains streams; streams that are alternately turbid torrents and mere dwindling threads of water. The great stretches of natural pasture are broken by gray sage-brush plains, and tracts of strangely shaped and colored Bad Lands; sun-scorched wastes in summer, and in winter arctic in their iron desolation. Beyond the plains rise the Rocky Mountains, their flanks covered with coniferous woods; but the trees are small, and do not ordinarily grow very closely together. Towards the north the forest becomes denser, and the peaks higher; and glaciers creep down towards the valleys from the fields of everlasting snow. The brooks are brawling, trout-filled torrents; the swift rivers foam over rapid and cataract, on their way to one or the other of the two great oceans.

Southwest of the Rockies evil and terrible deserts stretch for leagues and leagues, mere waterless wastes of sandy plain and barren mountain, broken here and there by narrow strips of fertile ground. Rain rarely falls, and there are no clouds to dim the brazen sun. The rivers run in deep canyons, or are swallowed by the burning sand; the smaller watercourses are dry throughout the greater part of the year.

Beyond this desert region rise the sunny Sierras of California, with their flower-clad slopes and groves of giant trees; and north of them, along the coast, the rain-shrouded mountain chains of Oregon and Washington, matted with the towering growth of the mighty evergreen forest.

The white hunters, who from time to time first penetrated the different parts of this wilderness, found themselves in such hunting grounds as those wherein, long ages before, their Old-World forefathers had dwelt; and the game they chased was much the same as that their lusty barbarian ancestors followed, with weapons of bronze and of iron, in the dim years before history dawned. As late as the end of the seventeenth century the turbulent village nobles of Lithuania and Livonia hunted the bear, the bison, the elk, the wolf, and the stag, and hung the spoils in their smoky wooden palaces; and so, two hundred years later, the free hunters of Montana, in the interludes between hazardous mining quests and bloody Indian campaigns, hunted game almost or quite the same in kind, through the cold mountain forests surrounding the Yellowstone and Flathead lakes, and decked their log cabins and ranch houses with the hides and horns of the slaughtered beasts.

Zoölogically speaking, the north temperate zones of the Old and New Worlds are very similar, differing from one another much less than they do from the various regions south of them, or than these regions differ among themselves. The untrodden American wilderness resembles both in game and physical character the forests, the mountains, and the steppes of the Old World as it was at the beginning of our era. Great woods of pine and fir, birch and beech, oak and chestnut; streams where the chief game fish are spotted trout and silvery salmon; grouse of various kinds as the most common game birds; all these the hunter finds as characteristic of the New World as of the Old. So it is with most of the beasts of the chase, and so also with the fur-bearing animals that furnish to the trapper alike his life work and his means of livelihood. The bear, wolf, bison, moose, caribou, wapiti, deer, and bighorn, the lynx, fox, wolverine, sable, mink, ermine, beaver, badger, and otter of both worlds are either identical or more or less closely kin to one another. Sometimes of the two forms, that found in the Old World is the largest. Perhaps more often the reverse is true, the American beast being superior in size. This is markedly the case with the wapiti, which is merely a giant brother of the European stag, exactly as the fisher is merely a very large cousin of the European sable or marten. The extraordinary prong-buck, the only hollow-horned ruminant which sheds its horns annually, is a distant representative of the Old-World antelopes of the steppes; the queer white antelope-goat has for its nearest kinsfolk certain Himalayan species. Of the animals commonly known to our hunters and trappers, only a few, such as the cougar, peccary, raccoon, possum (and among birds the wild turkey), find their nearest representatives and type forms in tropical America.

Of course this general resemblance does not mean identity. The differences in plant life and animal life, no less than in the physical features of the land, are sufficiently marked to give the American wilderness a character distinctly its own. Some of the most characteristic of the woodland animals, some of those which have most vividly impressed themselves on the imagination of the hunters and pioneer settlers, are the very ones which have no Old-World representatives. The wild turkey is in every way the king of American game birds. Among the small beasts the coon and the possum are those which have left the deepest traces in the humbler lore of the frontier; exactly as the cougar—usually under the name of panther or mountain lion—is a favorite figure in the wilder hunting tales. Nowhere else is there any-thing to match the wealth of the eastern hardwood forests, in number, variety, and beauty of trees; nowhere else is it possible to find conifers approaching in size the giant redwoods and sequoias of the Pacific slope. Nature here is generally on a larger scale than in the Old-World home of our race. The lakes are like inland seas, the rivers like arms of the sea. Among stupendous mountain chains there are valleys and canyons of fathomless depth and incredible beauty and majesty. There are tropical swamps, and sad, frozen marshes; deserts and Death Val-leys, weird and evil, and the strange wonderland of the Wyoming geyser region. The waterfalls are rivers rushing over precipices; the prairies seem without limit, and the forest never ending.

At the time when we first became a nation, nine tenths of the terri-tory now included within the limits of the United States was wilder-ness. It was during the stirring and troubled years immediately preceding the outbreak of the Revolution that the most adventurous hunters, the vanguard of the hardy army of pioneer settlers, first crossed the Alleghanies, and roamed far and wide through the lonely, danger-haunted forests which filled the No-man's-land lying between the Tennessee and the Ohio. They waged ferocious warfare with Shawnee and Wyandott and wrought huge havoc among the herds of game with which the forests teemed. While the first Continental Con-gress was still sitting, Daniel Boone, the archetype of the American hunter, was leading his bands of tall backwoods riflemen to settle in the beautiful country of Kentucky, where the red and the white war-riors strove with such obstinate rage that both races alike grew to know it as "the dark and bloody ground."

Boone and his fellow-hunters were the heralds of the oncoming civilization, the pioneers in that conquest of the wilderness which has at last been practically achieved in our own day. Where they pitched their camps and built their log huts or stockaded hamlets, towns grew up, and men who were tillers of the soil, not mere wilderness wander-ers, thronged in to take and hold the land. Then, ill-at-ease among the settlements for which they had themselves made ready the way, and fretted even by the slight restraints of the rude and uncouth semi-civilization of the border, the restless hunters moved onward into the yet unbroken wilds where the game dwelt and the red tribes marched forever to war and hunting. Their untamable souls ever found something congenial and beyond measure attractive in the lawless freedom of the lives of the very savages against whom they warred so bitterly.

Step by step, often leap by leap, the frontier of settlement was pushed westward; and ever from before its advance fled the warrior tribes of the red men and the scarcely less intractable array of white Indian fighters and game hunters. When the Revolutionary war was at its height, George Rogers Clarke, himself a mighty hunter of the old backwoods type, led his handful of hunter-soldiers to the conquest of the French towns of the Illinois. This was but one of the many notable feats of arms performed by the wild soldiery of the backwoods. Clad in their fringed and tasselled hunting shirts of buckskin or homespun, with coonskin caps and deer-hide leggings and moccasins, with tomahawk and scalping knife thrust into their bead-worked belts, and long rifles in hand, they fought battle after battle of the most bloody character, both against the Indians, as at the Great Kanawha, at the Fallen Timbers, and at Tippecanoe, and against more civilized foes, as at King's Mountain, New Orleans, and the River Thames.

Soon after the beginning of the present century Louisiana fell into our hands, and the most daring hunters and explorers pushed through the forests of the Mississippi valley to the great plains, steered across these vast seas of grass to the Rocky Mountains, and then through their rugged defiles onwards to the Pacific Ocean. In every work of exploration, and in all the earlier battles with the original lords of the western and southwestern lands, whether Indian or Mexican, the adventurous hunters played the leading part; while close behind came the swarm of hard, dogged, border-farmers,—a masterful race, good fighters and good breeders, as all masterful races must be.

Very characteristic in its way was the career of quaint, honest, fearless Davy Crockett, the Tennessee rifleman and Whig Congressman, perhaps the best shot in all our country, whose skill in the use of his favorite weapon passed into a proverb, and who ended his days by a hero's death in the ruins of the Alamo. An even more notable man was another mighty hunter, Houston, who when a boy ran away to the Indians; who while still a lad returned to his own people to serve under Andrew Jackson in the campaigns which that greatest of all the backwoods leaders waged against the Creeks, the Spaniards, and the

British. He was wounded at the storming of one of the strongholds of Red Eagle's doomed warriors, and returned to his Tennessee home to rise to high civil honor, and become the foremost man of his State. Then, while Governor of Tennessee, in a sudden fit of moody anger, and of mad longing for the unfettered life of the wilderness, he abandoned his office, his people, and his race, and fled to the Cherokees beyond the Mississippi. For years he lived as one of their chiefs; until one day, as he lay in ignoble ease and sloth, a rider from the south, from the rolling plains of the San Antonio and Brazos, brought word that the Texans were up, and in doubtful struggle striving to wrest their freedom from the lancers and carbineers of Santa Anna. Then his dark soul flamed again into burning life; riding by night and day he joined the risen Texans, was hailed by them as a heaven-sent leader, and at the San Jacinto led them on to the overthrow of the Mexican host. Thus the stark hunter, who had been alternately Indian fighter and Indian chief, became the President of the new Republic, and, after its admission into the United States, a Senator at Washington; and, to his high honor, he remained to the end of his days staunchly loyal to the flag of the Union.

By the time that Crockett fell, and Houston became the darling leader of the Texans, the typical hunter and Indian fighter had ceased to be a backwoodsman; he had become a plains-man, or mountain-man; for the frontier, east of which he never willingly went, had been pushed beyond the Mississippi. Restless, reckless, and hardy, he spent years of his life in lonely wanderings through the Rockies as a trapper; he guarded the slow-moving caravans, which for purposes of trade journeyed over the dangerous Santa Fé trail; he guided the large parties of frontier settlers who, driving before them their cattle, with all their household goods in their white-topped wagons, spent perilous months and seasons on their weary way to Oregon or California. Joining in bands, the stalwart, skin-clad riflemen waged ferocious war on the Indians scarcely more savage than themselves, or made long raids for plunder and horses against the outlying Mexican settlements. The best, the bravest, the most modest of them all was the renowned Kit Carson. He was not only a mighty hunter, a daring fighter, a finder of trails, and maker of roads through the unknown, untrodden wilderness, but also a real leader of men. Again and again he crossed and re-crossed the continent, from the Mississippi to the Pacific; he guided many of the earliest military and exploring expeditions of the United States Government; he himself led the troops in victorious campaigns against Apache and Navahoe; and in the Civil War he was made a colonel of the Federal army.

After him came many other hunters. Most were pure-blooded Americans, but many were Creole Frenchmen, Mexicans, or even members of the so-called civilized Indian tribes, notably the Delawares. Wide were their wanderings, many their strange adventures in the chase, bitter their unending warfare with the red lords of the land. Hither and thither they roamed, from the desolate, burning deserts of the Colorado to the grassy plains of the Upper Missouri; from the rolling Texas prairies, bright beneath their sunny skies, to the high snow peaks of the northern Rockies, or the giant pine forests, and soft rainy weather, of the coasts of Puget Sound. Their main business was trapping, furs being the only articles yielded by the wilderness, as they knew it, which were both valuable and portable. These early hunters were all trappers likewise, and, indeed, used their rifles only to procure meat or repel attacks. The chief of the fur-bearing animals they followed was the beaver, which abounded in the streams of the plains and mountains; in the far north they also trapped otter, mink, sable, and fisher. They married squaws from among the Indian tribes with which they happened for the moment to be at peace; they acted as scouts for the United States troops in their campaigns against the tribes with which they happened to be at war.

Soon after the Civil War the life of these hunters, taken as a class, entered on its final stage. The Pacific coast was already fairly well settled, and there were a few mining camps in the Rockies; but most of this Rocky Mountains region, and the entire stretch of plains country proper, the vast belt of level or rolling grass land lying between the Rio Grande and the Saskatchewan, still remained primeval wilderness, inhabited only by roving hunters and formidable tribes of Indian nomads, and by the huge herds of game on which they preyed. Beaver swarmed in the streams and yielded a rich harvest to the trapper; but trapping was no longer the mainstay of the adventurous plainsmen. Foremost among the beasts of the chase, on account of its numbers, its size, and its economic importance, was the bison or American buffalo:

its innumerable multitudes darkened the limitless prairies. As the transcontinental railroads were pushed towards completion, and the tide of settlement rolled onwards with ever increasing rapidity, buffalo robes became of great value. The hunters forthwith turned their attention mainly to the chase of the great clumsy beasts, slaughtering them by hundreds of thousands for their hides; sometimes killing them on horseback, but more often on foot, by still-hunting, with the heavy long-range Sharp's rifle. Throughout the fifteen years during which this slaughter lasted, a succession of desperate wars was waged with the banded tribes of the Horse Indians. All the time, in unending succession, long trains of big white-topped wagons crept slowly westward across the prairies, marking the steady oncoming of the frontier settlers.

By the close of 1883 the last buffalo herd was destroyed. The beaver were trapped out of all the streams, or their numbers so thinned that it no longer paid to follow them. The last formidable Indian war had been brought to a successful close. The flood of the incoming whites had risen over the land; tongues of settlement reached from the Mississippi to the Rocky Mountains, and from the Rocky Mountains to the Pacific. The frontier had come to an end; it had vanished. With it vanished also the old race of wilderness hunters, the men who spent all their days in the lonely wilds, and who killed game as their sole means of livelihood. Great stretches of wilderness still remain in the Rocky Mountains, and here and there in the plains country, exactly as much smaller tracts of wild land are to be found in the Alleghanies and northern New York and New England; and on these tracts occasional hunters and trappers still linger; but as a distinctive class, with a peculiar and important position in American life, they no longer exist.

* * *

THE KLONDIKE

Edwin Arlington Robinson

Never mind the day we left, or the way the women clung
    to us;
All we need now is the last way they looked at us.
Never mind the twelve men there amid the cheering—
Twelve men or one man, 't will soon be all the same;
For this is what we know: we are five men together,
Five left o' twelve men to find the golden river.

Far we came to find it out, but the place was here for
    all of us;
Far, far we came, and here we have the last of us.
We that were the front men, we that would be early,
We that had the faith, and the triumph in our eyes:
We that had the wrong road, twelve men together,—
Singing when the devil sang to find the golden river.

Say the gleam was not for us, but never say we doubted it;
Say the wrong road was right before we followed it.
We that were the front men, fit for all forage,—
Say that while we dwindle we are front men still;
For this is what we know to-night: we're starving here
    together—
Starving on the wrong road to find the golden river.

Wrong, we say, but wait a little: hear him in the corner
    there;
He knows more than we, and he'll tell us if we listen
    there—
He that fought the snow-sleep less than all the others
Stays awhile yet, and he knows where he stays:
Foot and hand a frozen clout, brain a freezing feather,
Still he's here to talk with us and to the golden river.

"Flow," he says, "and flow along, but you cannot flow away
       from us;
All the world's ice will never keep you far from us;
Every man that heeds your call takes the way that leads him—
The one way that's his way, and lives his own life:
Starve or laugh, the game goes on, and on goes the river;
Gold or no, they go their way—twelve men together.

"Twelve," he says, "who sold their shame for a lure you call
       too fair for them—
You that laugh and flow to the same word that urges them:
Twelve who left the old town shining in the sunset,
Left the weary street and the small safe days:
Twelve who knew but one way out, wide the way or narrow:
Twelve who took the frozen chance and laid their lives
       on yellow.

"Flow by night and flow by day, nor ever once be seen by
       them;
Flow, freeze, and flow, till time shall hide the bones of them;
Laugh and wash their names away, leave them all forgotten,
Leave the old town to crumble where it sleeps;
Leave it there as they have left it, shining in the valley,—
Leave the town to crumble down and let the women marry.

"Twelve of us or five," he says, "we know the night is on
       us now:
Five while we last, and we may as well be thinking now:
Thinking each his own thought, knowing, when the light
       comes,
Five left or none left, the game will not be lost.
Crouch or sleep, we go the way, the last way together:
Five or none, the game goes on, and on goes the river.

"For after all that we have done and all that we have failed
       to do,
Life will be life and the world will have its work to do:

Every man who follows us will heed in his own fashion
The calling and the warning and the friends who do not
    know:
Each will hold an icy knife to punish his heart's lover,
And each will go the frozen way to find the golden river."

There you hear him, all he says, and the last we'll ever get
    from him.
Now he wants to sleep, and that will be the best for him.
Let him have his own way—no, you need n't shake him—
Your own turn will come, so let the man sleep.
For this is what we know: we are stalled here together—
Hands and feet and hearts of us, to find the golden river.

And there's a quicker way than sleep? . . . Never mind the
    looks of him:
All he needs now is a finger on the eyes of him.
You there on the left hand, reach a little over—
Shut the stars away, or he'll see them all night:
He'll see them all night and he'll see them all to-morrow,
Crawling down the frozen sky, cold and hard and yellow.

Won't you move an inch or two—to keep the stars away
    from him?
—No, he won't move, and there's no need of asking him.
Never mind the twelve men, never mind the women;
Three while we last, we'll let them all go;
And we'll hold our thoughts north while we starve here
    together,
Looking each his own way to find the golden river.

DISSENT

The concept of freedom of expression is dearly held, even if it has sometimes been more valued in theory than in practice. These few selections concern slavery and opposition to it. In the first, the poet John Greenleaf Whittier (1807–1892) lauds his fellow abolitionist William Lloyd Garrison, although the two later fell out. The most famous slave narrative is that of Frederick Douglass, who was born in Tuckahoe, Maryland, in slavery in 1817 and escaped to Philadelphia in 1838. He married and moved to New Bedford, Massachusetts, where he encountered Garrison's paper, The Liberator, *and campaigned brilliantly for the Massachusetts Anti-Slavery Society. He wrote his* Narrative *in 1845, and in 1847 he began to publish his own abolitionist paper. During the Civil War he served as an adviser to President Lincoln; afterward he held a number of government posts. He died in 1895. Henry David Thoreau (1817–1862) spent a night in jail in 1846 to protest against slavery. He wrote* Civil Disobedience *in 1849 to explain his motives. Thoreau met Captain John Brown in 1847 and later wrote "A Plea for Captain John Brown" in his defense. Ralph Waldo Emerson's appeal for the life of Brown is included here. The Transcendental philosopher Emerson (1803–1882) lectured extensively against slavery. He delivered this speech in Boston on November 18, 1858, when the militant antislavery campaigner John Brown was under sentence of death for his raid on the federal armory at Harpers Ferry. He was executed two weeks later.* The Souls of Black Folk *(1903) was just one of the works of pioneering sociologist W.E.B. Du Bois (1868–1963). In his long and eventful life, Du Bois was a founder of the National Association for the Advancement of Colored Peoples (the NAACP) and long-time editor of its magazine,* The Crisis. *He eventually joined the Communist Party and moved to Ghana, renouncing his American citizenship.*

To William Lloyd Garrison

John Greenleaf Whittier

Champion of those who groan beneath
   Oppression's iron hand:
In view of penury, hate, and death,
   I see thee fearless stand.
Still bearing up thy lofty brow,
   In the steadfast strength of truth,
In manhood sealing well the vow
   And promise of thy youth.

Go on, for thou hast chosen well;
   On in the strength of God!
Long as one human heart shall swell
   Beneath the tyrant's rod.
Speak in a slumbering nation's ear,
   As thou hast ever spoken,
Until the dead in sin shall hear,
   The fetter's link be broken!

I love thee with a brother's love,
   I feel my pulses thrill,
To mark thy spirit soar above
   The cloud of human ill.
My heart hath leaped to answer thine,
   And echo back thy words,
As leaps the warrior's at the shine
   And flash of kindred swords!

They tell me thou art rash and vain,
   A searcher after fame;
That thou art striving but to gain
   A long-enduring name;
That thou hast nerved the Afric's hand

And steeled the Afric's heart,
To shake aloft his vengeful brand,
And rend his chain apart.

Have I not known thee well, and read
Thy mighty purpose long?
And watched the trials which have made
Thy human spirit strong?
And shall the slanderer's demon breath
Avail with one like me,
To dim the sunshine of my faith
And earnest trust in thee?

Go on, the dagger's point may glare
Amid thy pathway's gloom;
The fate which sternly threatens there
Is glorious martyrdom!
Then onward with a martyr's zeal;
And wait thy sure reward
When man to man no more shall kneel,
And God alone be Lord!

FROM

NARRATIVE OF THE LIFE OF FREDERICK DOUGLASS, AN AMERICAN SLAVE

I was born in Tuckahoe, near Hillsborough, and about twelve miles from Easton, in Talbot county, Maryland. I have no accurate knowledge of my age, never having seen any authentic record containing it. By far the larger part of the slaves know as little of their ages as horses know of theirs, and it is the wish of most masters within my knowledge to keep their slaves thus ignorant. I do not remember to have ever met a slave who could tell of his birthday. They seldom come nearer to it than planting-time, harvest-time, cherry-time, spring-time, or fall-time. A want of information concerning my own was a source of unhappiness to me even during childhood. The white children could tell their ages. I could not tell why I ought to be deprived of the same privilege. I was not allowed to make any inquiries of my master concerning it. He deemed all such inquiries on the part of a slave improper and impertinent, and evidence of a restless spirit. The nearest estimate I can give makes me now between twenty-seven and twenty-eight years of age. I come to this, from hearing my master say, some time during 1835, I was about seventeen years old.

My mother was named Harriet Bailey. She was the daughter of Isaac and Betsey Bailey, both colored, and quite dark. My mother was of a darker complexion than either my grandmother or grandfather.

My father was a white man. He was admitted to be such by all I ever heard speak of my parentage. The opinion was also whispered that my master was my father; but of the correctness of this opinion, I know nothing; the means of knowing was withheld from me. My mother and I were separated when I was but an infant—before I knew her as my mother. It is a common custom, in the part of Maryland from which I ran away, to part children from their mothers at a very early age. Frequently, before the child has reached its twelfth month, its mother is taken from it, and hired out on some farm a considerable distance off, and the child is placed under the care of an old woman, too old for field labor. For what this separation is done, I do not know, unless it be to hinder the development of the child's affection toward its mother, and to blunt and destroy the natural affection of the mother for the child. This is the inevitable result.

I never saw my mother, to know her as such, more than four or five times in my life; and each of those times was very short in duration, and at night. She was hired by a Mr. Stewart, who lived about twelve miles from my home. She made her journeys to see me in the night, travelling the whole distance on foot, after the performance of her day's work. She was a field hand, and a whipping is the penalty of not being in the field at sunrise, unless a slave has special permission from his or her master to the contrary—a permission which they seldom get, and one that gives to him that gives it the proud name of being a kind master. I do not recollect of ever seeing my mother by the light of day. She was with me in the night. She would lie down with me, and get me to sleep, but long before I waked she was gone. Very little communication ever took place between us. Death soon ended what little we could have while she lived, and with it her hardships and suffering. She died when I was about seven years old, on one of my master's farms, near Lee's Mill. I was not allowed to be present during her illness, at her death, or burial. She was gone long before I knew any thing about it. Never having enjoyed, to any considerable extent, her soothing presence, her tender and watchful care, I received the tidings of her death with much the same emotions I should have probably felt at the death of a stranger.

Called thus suddenly away, she left me without the slightest intimation of who my father was. The whisper that my master was my father, may or may not be true; and, true or false, it is of but little consequence to my purpose whilst the fact remains, in all its glaring odiousness, that slaveholders have ordained, and by law established, that the children of slave women shall in all cases follow the condition of their mothers; and this is done too obviously to administer to their own lusts, and make a gratification of their wicked desires profitable as well as pleasurable; for by this cunning arrangement, the slaveholder, in cases not a few, sustains to his slaves the double relation of master and father.

* * *

I have had two masters. My first master's name was Anthony. I do not remember his first name. He was generally called Captain Anthony—a title which, I presume, he acquired by sailing a craft on the Chesapeake Bay. He was not considered a rich slaveholder. He owned two or three farms, and about thirty slaves. His farms and slaves were under the care of an overseer. The overseer's name was Plummer. Mr. Plummer was a miserable drunkard, a profane swearer, and a savage monster. He always went armed with a cowskin and a heavy cudgel. I have known him to cut and slash the women's heads so horribly, that even master would be enraged at his cruelty, and would threaten to whip him if he did not mind himself. Master, however, was not a humane slaveholder. It required extraordinary barbarity on the part of an overseer to affect him. He was a cruel man, hardened by a long life of slaveholding. He would at times seem to take great pleasure in whipping a slave. I have often been awakened at the dawn of day by the most heart-rending shrieks of an own aunt of mine, whom he used to tie up to a joist, and whip upon her naked back till she was literally covered with blood. No words, no tears, no prayers, from his gory victim, seemed to move his iron heart from its bloody purpose. The louder she screamed, the harder he whipped; and where the blood ran fastest, there he whipped longest. He would whip her to make her scream, and whip her to make her hush; and not until overcome by fatigue, would he cease to swing the blood-clotted cowskin. I remember the first time I ever witnessed this horrible exhibition. I was quite a child, but I well remember it. I never shall forget it whilst I remember any thing. It was the first of a long series of such outrages, of which I was doomed to be a witness and a participant. It struck me with awful force. It was the blood-stained gate, the entrance to the hell of slavery, through which I was about to pass. It was a most terrible spectacle. I wish I could commit to paper the feelings with which I beheld it.

This occurrence took place very soon after I went to live with my old master, and under the following circumstances. Aunt Hester went out one night,—where or for what I do not know,—and happened to be absent when my master desired her presence. He had ordered her not to go out evenings, and warned her that she must never let him catch her in company with a young man, who was paying attention to her belonging to Colonel Lloyd. The young man's name was Ned Roberts, generally called Lloyd's Ned. Why master was so careful of her, may be safely left to conjecture. She was a woman of noble form, and of graceful proportions, having very few equals, and fewer superiors, in personal appearance, among the colored or white women of our neighborhood.

Aunt Hester had not only disobeyed his orders in going out, but had been found in company with Lloyd's Ned; which circumstance, I found, from what he said while whipping her, was the chief offence. Had he been a man of pure morals himself, he might have been thought interested in protecting the innocence of my aunt; but those who knew him will not suspect him of any such virtue. Before he commenced whipping Aunt Hester, he took her into the kitchen, and stripped her from neck to waist, leaving her neck, shoulders, and back, entirely naked. He then told her to cross her hands, calling her at the same time a d——d b——h. After crossing her hands, he tied them with a strong rope, and led her to a stool under a large hook in the joist, put in for the purpose. He made her get upon the stool, and tied her hands to the hook. She now stood fair for his infernal purpose. Her arms were stretched up at their full length, so that she stood upon the ends of her toes. He then said to her, "Now, you d——d b——h, I'll learn you how to disobey my orders!" and after rolling up his sleeves, he commenced to lay on the heavy cowskin, and soon the warm, red blood (amid heart-rending shrieks from her, and horrid oaths from him) came dripping to the floor. I was so terrified and horror-stricken at the sight, that I hid myself in a closet, and dared not venture out till long after the bloody transaction was over. I expected it would be my turn next. It was all new to me. I had never seen any thing like it before. I had always lived with my grand-mother on the outskirts of the plantation, where she was put to raise the children of the younger women. I had therefore been, until now, out of the way of the bloody scenes that often occurred on the plantation.

FROM

CIVIL DISOBEDIENCE

Henry David Thoreau

I heartily accept the motto,—"That government is best which governs least;" and I should like to see it acted up to more rapidly and systematically. Carried out, it finally amounts to this, which also I believe,—"That government is best which governs not at all;" and when men are prepared for it, that will be the kind of government which they will have. Government is at best but an expedient; but most governments are usually, and all governments are sometimes, inexpedient. The objections which have been brought against a standing army, and they are many and weighty, and deserve to prevail, may also at last be brought against a standing government. The standing army is only an arm of the standing government. The government itself, which is only the mode which the people have chosen to execute their will, is equally liable to be abused and perverted before the people can act through it. Witness the present Mexican war, the work of comparatively a few individuals using the standing government as their tool; for, in the outset, the people would not have consented to this measure.

This American government,—what is it but a tradition, though a recent one, endeavoring to transmit itself unimpaired to posterity, but each instant losing some of its integrity? It has not the vitality and force of a single living man; for a single man can bend it to his will. It is a sort of wooden gun to the people themselves. But it is not the less necessary for this; for the people must have some complicated machinery or other, and hear its din, to satisfy that idea of government which they have. Governments show thus how successfully men can be imposed on, even impose on themselves, for their own advantage. It is excellent, we must all allow. Yet this government never of itself furthered any enterprise, but by the alacrity with which it got out of its way. *It* does not keep the country free. *It* does not settle the West. *It* does not educate. The character inherent in the American people has done all that has been accomplished; and it would have done somewhat more, if the government had not sometimes got in its way. For government is an expedient by which men would fain succeed in letting one another alone; and, as has been said, when it is most expedient, the governed are most let alone by it. Trade and commerce, if they were not made of India-rubber, would never manage to bounce over the obstacles which legislators are continually putting in their way; and, if one were to judge these men wholly by the effects of their actions and not partly by their intentions, they would deserve to be classed and punished with those mischievous persons who put obstructions on the railroads.

But, to speak practically and as a citizen, unlike those who call themselves no-government men, I ask for, not at once no government, but *at once* a better government. Let every man make known what kind of government would command his respect, and that will be one step toward obtaining it.

After all, the practical reason why, when the power is once in the hands of the people, a majority are permitted, and for a long period continue, to rule is not because they are most likely to be in the right, nor because this seems fairest to the minority, but because they are physically the strongest. But a government in which the majority rule in all cases cannot be based on justice, even as far as men understand it. Can there not be a government in which majorities do not virtually decide right and wrong, but conscience?—in which majorities decide only those questions to which the rule of expediency is applicable? Must the citizen ever for a moment, or in the least degree, resign his conscience to the legislator? Why has every man a conscience, then? I think that we should be men first, and subjects afterward. It is not desirable to cultivate a respect for the law, so much as for the right. The only obligation which I have a right to assume is to do at any time what I think right. It is truly enough said, that a corporation has no conscience; but a corporation of conscientious men is a corporation *with* a conscience. Law never made men a whit more just; and, by means of their respect for it, even the well-disposed are daily made the agents of injustice. A common and natural result of an undue respect for law is, that you may see a file of soldiers, colonel, captain, corporal, privates, powder-monkeys, and all, marching in admirable order over hill and dale to the wars, against their wills, ay, against their common sense and consciences, which makes it very steep marching indeed, and produces a palpitation of the heart. They have no doubt that it is a damnable business in which they are concerned; they are all peaceably inclined. Now, what are they? Men at all? or small movable forts and magazines, at the service of some unscrupulous man in power? Visit the Navy-Yard, and behold a marine, such a man as an American government can make, or such as it can make a man with its black arts,—a mere shadow and reminiscence of humanity, a man laid out alive and standing, and already, as one may say, buried under arms with funeral accompaniments, though it may be,—

"Not a drum was heard, not a funeral note,
　As his corse to the rampart we hurried;
Not a soldier discharged his farewell shot
　O'er the grave where our hero we buried."

The mass of men serve the state thus, not as men mainly, but as machines, with their bodies. They are the standing army, and the militia, jailors, constables, posse comitatus, etc. In most cases there is no free exercise whatever of the judgment or of the moral sense; but they put themselves on a level with wood and earth and stones; and wooden men can perhaps be manufactured that will serve the purpose as well. Such command no more respect than men of straw or a lump of dirt. They have the same sort of worth only as horses and dogs. Yet such as these even are commonly esteemed good citizens. Others—as most legislators, politicians, lawyers, ministers, and office-holders—serve the state chiefly with their heads; and, as they rarely make any moral distinctions, they are as likely to serve the Devil, without *intending* it, as God. A very few, as heroes, patriots, martyrs, reformers in the great sense, and *men,* serve the state with their consciences also, and so necessarily resist it for the most part; and they are commonly treated as enemies by it. A wise man will only be useful as a man, and will not submit to be "clay," and "stop a hole to keep the wind away," but leave that office to his dust at least:—

> "I am too high-born to be propertied,
>   To be a secondary at control,
>   Or useful serving-man and instrument
>   To any sovereign state throughout the world."

He who gives himself entirely to his fellow-men appears to them useless and selfish; but he who gives himself partially to them is pronounced a benefactor and philanthropist.

How does it become a man to behave toward this American government to-day? I answer, that he cannot without disgrace be associated with it. I cannot for an instant recognize that political organization as *my* government which is the *slave's* government also.

All men recognize the right of revolution; that is, the right to refuse allegiance to, and to resist, the government, when its tyranny or its inefficiency are great and unendurable. But almost all say that such is not the case now. But such was the case, they think, in the Revolution of '75. If one were to tell me that this was a bad government because it taxed certain foreign commodities brought to its ports, it is most probable that I should not make an ado about it, for I can do without them. All machines have their friction; and possibly this does enough good to counterbalance the evil. At any rate, it is a great evil to make a stir about it. But when the friction comes to have its machine, and oppression and robbery are organized, I say, let us not have such a machine any longer. In other words, when a sixth of the population of a nation which has undertaken to be the refuge of liberty are slaves, and a whole country is unjustly overrun and conquered by a foreign army, and subjected to military law, I think that it is not too soon for honest men to rebel and revolutionize. What makes this duty the more urgent is the fact that the country so overrun is not our own, but ours is the invading army.

* * *

JOHN BROWN

Ralph Waldo Emerson

Mr. Chairman, and Fellow Citizens: I share the sympathy and sorrow which brought us together. Gentlemen who have preceded me have well said that no wall of separation could here exist. This commanding event which has brought us together, eclipses all others which have occurred for a long time in our history, and I am very glad to see that this sudden interest in the hero of Harper's Ferry has provoked an extreme curiosity in all parts of the Republic, in regard to the details of his history. Every anecdote is eagerly sought, and I do not wonder that gentlemen find traits of relation readily between him and themselves. One finds a relation in the church, another in the profession, another in the place of his birth. He was happily a representative of the American Republic. Captain John Brown is a farmer, the fifth in descent from Peter Brown, who came to Plymouth in the Mayflower, in 1620. All the six have been farmers. His grandfather, of Simsbury, in Connecticut, was a captain in the Revolution. His father, largely interested as a raiser of stock, became a contractor to supply the army with beef, in the war of 1812, and our Captain John Brown, then a boy, with his father was present and witnessed the surrender of General Hull. He cherishes a great respect for his father, as a man of strong character, and his respect is probably just. For himself, he is so transparent that all men see him through. He is a man to make friends wherever on earth courage and integrity are esteemed, the rarest of heroes, a pure idealist, with no by-ends of his own. Many of you have seen him, and every one who has heard him speak has been impressed alike by his simple, artless goodness, joined with his sublime courage. He joins that perfect Puritan faith which brought his fifth ancestor to Plymouth Rock with his grandfather's ardor in the Revolution. He believes in two articles—two instruments, shall I say?—the Golden Rule and the Declaration of Independence; and he used this expression in conversation here concerning them, "Better that a whole generation of men, women and children should pass away by a violent death than that one word of either should be violated in this country." There is a Unionist—there is a strict constructionist for you. He believes in the Union of the States, and he conceives that the only obstruction to the Union is Slavery, and for that reason, as a patriot, he works for its abolition. The governor of Virginia has pronounced his eulogy in a manner that discredits the moderation of our timid parties. His own speeches to the court have interested the nation in him. What magnanimity, and what innocent pleading, as of childhood! You remember his words: "If I had interfered in behalf of the rich, the powerful, the intelligent, the so-called great, or any of their friends, parents, wives or children, it would all have been right. But I believe that to have interfered as I have done, for the despised poor, was not wrong, but right."

It is easy to see what a favorite he will be with history, which plays such pranks with temporary reputations. Nothing can resist the sympathy which all elevated minds must feel with Brown, and through them the whole civilized world; and if he must suffer, he must drag official gentlemen into an immortality most undesirable, of which they have already some disagreeable forebodings. Indeed, it is the *reductio ad absurdum* of Slavery, when the governor of Virginia is forced to hang a man whom he declares to be a man of the most integrity, truthfulness and courage he has ever met. Is that the kind of man the gallows is built for? It were bold to affirm that there is within that broad commonwealth, at this moment, another citizen as worthy to live, and as deserving of all public and private honor, as this poor prisoner.

But we are here to think of relief for the family of John Brown. To my eyes, that family looks very large and very needy of relief. It comprises his brave fellow sufferers in the Charlestown Jail; the fugitives still hunted in the mountains of Virginia and Pennsylvania; the sympathizers with him in all the states; and, I may say, almost every man who loves the Golden Rule and the Declaration of Independence, like him, and who sees what a tiger's thirst threatens him in the malignity of public sentiment in the slave states. It seems to me that a common feeling joins the people of Massachusetts with him.

I said John Brown was an idealist. He believed in his ideas to that extent that he existed to put them all into action; he said 'he did not believe in moral suasion, he believed in putting the thing through.' He saw how deceptive the forms are. We fancy, in Massachusetts, that we are free; yet it seems the government is quite unreliable. Great wealth, great population, men of talent in the executive, on the bench—all the forms right—and yet, life and freedom are not safe. Why? Because the judges rely on the forms, and do not, like John Brown, use their eyes to see the fact behind the forms. They assume that the United States can protect its witness or its prisoner. And in Massachusetts that is true, but the moment he is carried out of the bounds of Massachusetts, the United States, it is notorious, afford no protection at all; the government, the judges, are an envenomed party, and give such protection as they give in Utah to honest citizens, or in Kansas; such protection as they gave to their own Commodore Paulding, when he was simple enough to mistake the formal instructions of his government for their real meaning. The state judges fear collision between their two allegiances; but there are worse evils than collision; namely, the doing substantial injustice. A good man will see that the use of a judge is to secure good government, and where the citizen's weal is imperilled by abuse of the federal power, to use that arm which can secure it, viz., the local government. Had that been done on certain calamitous occasions, we should not have seen the honor of Massachusetts trailed in the dust, stained to all ages, once and again, by the ill-timed formalism of a venerable bench. If judges cannot find law enough to maintain the sovereignty of the state, and to protect the life and freedom of every inhabitant not a criminal, it is idle to compliment them as learned and venerable. What avails their learning or veneration? At a pinch, they are no more use than idiots. After the mischance they wring their hands, but they had better never have been born. A Vermont judge, Hutchinson, who has the Declaration of Independence in his heart; a

Wisconsin judge, who knows that laws are for the protection of citizens against kidnappers, is worth a court-house full of lawyers so idolatrous of forms as to let go the substance. Is any man in Massachusetts so simple as to believe that when a United States Court in Virginia, now, in its present reign of terror, sends to Connecticut, or New York, or Massachusetts, for a witness, it wants him for a witness? No; it wants him for a party; it wants him for meat to slaughter and eat. And your *habeas corpus* is, in any way in which it has been, or, I fear, is likely to be used, a nuisance, and not a protection; for it takes away his right reliance on himself, and the natural assistance of his friends and fellow citizens, by offering him a form which is a piece of paper.

But I am detaining the meeting on matters which others understand better. I hope, then, that, in administering relief to John Brown's family, we shall remember all those whom his fate concerns, all who are in sympathy with him, and not forget to aid him in the best way, by securing freedom and independence in Massachusetts.

FROM

THE SOULS OF BLACK FOLK

W.E.B. Du Bois

OF THE DAWN OF FREEDOM

The problem of the twentieth century is the problem of the color-line,—the relation of the darker to the lighter races of men in Asia and Africa, in America and the islands of the sea. It was a phase of this problem that caused the Civil War; and however much they who marched South and North in 1861 may have fixed on the technical points of union and local autonomy as a shibboleth, all nevertheless knew, as we know, that the question of Negro slavery was the real cause of the conflict. Curious it was, too, how this deeper question ever forced itself to the surface despite effort and disclaimer. No sooner had Northern armies touched Southern soil than this old question, newly guised, sprang from the earth,—What shall be done with Negroes? Peremptory military commands this way and that, could not answer the query; the Emancipation Proclamation seemed but to broaden and intensify the difficulties; and the War Amendments made the Negro problems of to-day.

It is the aim of this essay to study the period of history from 1861 to 1872 so far as it relates to the American Negro. In effect, this tale of the dawn of Freedom is an account of that government of men called the Freedmen's Bureau,—one of the most singular and interesting of the attempts made by a great nation to grapple with vast problems of race and social condition.

The war has naught to do with slaves, cried Congress, the President, and the Nation; and yet no sooner had the armies, East and West, penetrated Virginia and Tennessee than fugitive slaves appeared within their lines. They came at night, when the flickering camp-fires shone like vast unsteady stars along the black horizon: old men and thin, with gray and tufted hair; women with frightened eyes, dragging whimpering hungry children; men and girls, stalwart and gaunt,—a horde of starving vagabonds, homeless, helpless, and pitiable, in their dark distress. Two methods of treating these newcomers seemed equally logical to opposite sorts of minds. Ben Butler, in Virginia, quickly declared slave property contraband of war, and put the fugitives to work; while Fremont, in Missouri, declared the slaves free under martial law. Butler's action was approved, but Fremont's was hastily countermanded, and his successor, Halleck, saw things differently. "Hereafter," he commanded, "no slaves should be allowed to come into your lines at all; if any come without your knowledge, when owners call for them deliver them." Such a policy was difficult to enforce; some of the black refugees declared themselves freemen, others showed that their masters had deserted them, and still others were captured with forts and plantations. Evidently, too, slaves were a source of strength to the Confederacy, and were being used as laborers and producers. "They constitute a military resource," wrote Secretary Cameron, late in 1861; "and being such, that they should not be turned over to the enemy is too plain to discuss." So gradually the tone of the army chiefs changed; Congress forbade the rendition of fugitives, and Butler's "contrabands" were welcomed as military laborers. This complicated rather than solved the problem, for now the scattering fugitives became a steady stream, which flowed faster as the armies marched.

Then the long-headed man with care-chiselled face who sat in the White House saw the inevitable, and emancipated the slaves of rebels on New Year's, 1863. A month later Congress called earnestly for the Negro soldiers whom the act of July, 1862, had half grudgingly allowed to enlist. Thus the barriers were levelled and the deed was done. The stream of fugitives swelled to a flood, and anxious army officers kept inquiring: "What must be done with slaves, arriving almost daily? Are we to find food and shelter for women and children?"

It was a Pierce of Boston who pointed out the way, and thus became in a sense the founder of the Freedmen's Bureau. He was a firm friend of Secretary Chase; and when, in 1861, the care of slaves and abandoned lands devolved upon the Treasury officials, Pierce was specially detailed from the ranks to study the conditions. First, he cared for the refugees at Fortress Monroe; and then, after Sherman had captured Hilton Head, Pierce was sent there to found his Port Royal experiment of making free workingmen out of slaves. Before his experiment was barely started, however, the problem of the fugitives had assumed such proportions that it was taken from the hands of the over-burdened Treasury Department and given to the army officials. Already centres of massed freedmen were forming at Fortress Monroe, Washington, New Orleans, Vicksburg and Corinth, Columbus, Ky., and Cairo, Ill., as well as at Port Royal. Army chaplains found here new and fruitful fields; "superintendents of contrabands" multiplied, and some attempt at systematic work was made by enlisting the able-bodied men and giving work to the others.

Then came the Freedmen's Aid societies, born of the touching appeals from Pierce and from these other centres of distress. There was the American Missionary Association, sprung from the *Amistad,* and now full-grown for work; the various church organizations, the National Freedmen's Relief Association, the American Freedmen's Union, the Western Freedmen's Aid Commission,—in all fifty or more active organizations, which sent clothes, money, school-books, and teachers southward. All they did was needed, for the destitution of the freedmen was often reported as "too appalling for belief," and the situation was daily growing worse rather than better.

And daily, too, it seemed more plain that this was no ordinary matter of temporary relief, but a national crisis; for here loomed a labor problem of vast dimensions. Masses of Negroes stood idle, or, if they worked spasmodically, were never sure of pay; and if perchance they received pay, squandered the new thing thoughtlessly. In these and other ways were camp-life and the new liberty demoralizing the freedmen. The broader economic organization thus clearly demanded sprang up here and there as accident and local conditions determined.

Here it was that Pierce's Port Royal plan of leased plantations and guided workmen pointed out the rough way. In Washington the military governor, at the urgent appeal of the superintendent, opened confiscated estates to the cultivation of the fugitives, and there in the shadow of the dome gathered black farm villages. General Dix gave over estates to the freedmen of Fortress Monroe, and so on, South and West. The government and benevolent societies furnished the means of cultivation, and the Negro turned again slowly to work. The systems of control, thus started, rapidly grew, here and there, into strange little governments, like that of General Banks in Louisiana, with its ninety thousand black subjects, its fifty thousand guided laborers, and its annual budget of one hundred thousand dollars and more. It made out four thousand pay-rolls a year, registered all freedmen, inquired into grievances and redressed them, laid and collected taxes, and established a system of public schools. So, too, Colonel Eaton, the superintendent of Tennessee and Arkansas, ruled over one hundred thousand freedmen, leased and cultivated seven thousand acres of cotton land, and fed ten thousand paupers a year. In South Carolina was General Saxton, with his deep interest in black folk. He succeeded Pierce and the Treasury officials, and sold forfeited estates, leased abandoned plantations, encouraged schools, and received from Sherman, after that terribly picturesque march to the sea, thousands of the wretched camp followers.

Three characteristic things one might have seen in Sherman's raid through Georgia, which threw the new situation in shadowy relief: the Conqueror, the Conquered, and the Negro. Some see all significance in the grim front of the destroyer, and some in the bitter sufferers of the Lost Cause. But to me neither soldier nor fugitive speaks with so deep a meaning as that dark human cloud that clung like remorse on the rear of those swift columns, swelling at times to half their size, almost engulfing and choking them. In vain were they ordered back, in vain were bridges hewn from beneath their feet; on they trudged and writhed and surged, until they rolled into Savannah, a starved and naked horde of tens of thousands. There too came the characteristic military remedy: "The islands from Charleston south, the abandoned rice-fields along the rivers for thirty miles back from the sea, and the country bordering the St. John's River, Florida, are reserved and set apart for the settlement of Negroes now made free by act of war." So read the celebrated "Field-order Number Fifteen."

All these experiments, orders, and systems were bound to attract and perplex the government and the nation. Directly after the Emancipation Proclamation, Representative Eliot had introduced a bill creating a Bureau of Emancipation; but it was never reported. The following June a committee of inquiry, appointed by the Secretary of War, reported in favor of a temporary bureau for the "improvement, protection, and employment of refugee freedmen," on much the same lines as were afterwards followed. Petitions came in to President Lincoln from distinguished citizens and organizations, strongly urging a comprehensive and unified plan of dealing with the freedmen, under a bureau which should be "charged with the study of plans and execution of measures for easily guiding, and in every way judiciously and humanely aiding, the passage of our emancipated and yet to be emancipated blacks from the old condition of forced labor to their new state of voluntary industry."

Some half-hearted steps were taken to accomplish this, in part, by putting the whole matter again in charge of the special Treasury agents. Laws of 1863 and 1864 directed them to take charge of and lease abandoned lands for periods not exceeding twelve months, and to "provide in such leases, or otherwise, for the employment and general welfare" of the freedmen. Most of the army officers greeted this as a welcome relief from perplexing "Negro affairs," and Secretary Fessenden, July 29, 1864, issued an excellent system of regulations, which were afterward closely followed by General Howard. Under Treasury agents, large quantities of land were leased in the Mississippi Valley, and many Negroes were employed; but in August, 1864, the new regulations were suspended for reasons of "public policy," and the army was again in control.

Meanwhile Congress had turned its attention to the subject; and in March the House passed a bill by a majority of two establishing a Bureau for Freedmen in the War Department. Charles Sumner, who had charge of the bill in the Senate, argued that freedmen and abandoned lands ought to be under the same department, and reported a substitute for the House bill attaching the Bureau to the Treasury Department. This bill passed, but too late for action by the House. The debates wandered over the whole policy of the administration and the general question of slavery, without touching very closely the specific merits of the measure in hand. Then the national election took place; and the administration, with a vote of renewed confidence from the country, addressed itself to the matter more seriously. A conference between the two branches of Congress agreed upon a carefully drawn measure which contained the chief provisions of Sumner's bill, but made the proposed organization a department independent of both the War and the Treasury officials. The bill was conservative, giving the new department "general superintendence of all freedmen." Its purpose was to "establish regulations" for them, protect them, lease them lands, adjust their wages, and appear in civil and military courts as their "next friend." There were many limitations attached to the powers thus granted, and the organization was made permanent. Nevertheless, the Senate defeated the bill, and a new conference committee was appointed. This committee reported a new bill, February 28, which was whirled through just as the session closed, and became the act of 1865 establishing in the War Department a "Bureau of Refugees, Freedmen, and Abandoned Lands."

This last compromise was a hasty bit of legislation, vague and uncertain in outline. A Bureau was created, "to continue during the present War of Rebellion, and for one year thereafter," to which was given "the supervision and management of all abandoned lands and the control of all subjects relating to refugees and freedmen," under "such rules and regulations as may be presented by the head of the Bureau and approved by the President." A Commissioner, appointed by the President and Senate, was to control the Bureau, with an office force not exceeding ten clerks. The President might also appoint assistant commissioners in the seceded States, and to all these offices military officials might be detailed at regular pay. The Secretary of War could issue rations, clothing, and fuel to the destitute, and all abandoned property was placed in the hands of the Bureau for eventual lease and sale to ex-slaves in forty-acre parcels.

Thus did the United States government definitely assume charge of the emancipated Negro as the ward of the nation. It was a tremendous undertaking. Here at a stroke of the pen was erected a government of millions of men,—and not ordinary men either, but black men emasculated by a peculiarly complete system of slavery, centuries old; and now, suddenly, violently, they come into a new birthright, at a time of war and passion, in the midst of the stricken and embittered population of their former masters. Any man might well have hesitated to assume charge of such a work, with vast responsibilities, indefinite powers, and limited resources. Probably no one but a soldier would have answered such a call promptly; and, indeed, no one but a soldier could be called, for Congress had appropriated no money for salaries and expenses.

Less than a month after the weary Emancipator passed to his rest, his successor assigned Major-Gen. Oliver O. Howard to duty as Commissioner of the new Bureau. He was a Maine man, then only thirty-five years of age. He had marched with Sherman to the sea, had fought well at Gettysburg, and but the year before had been assigned to the command of the Department of Tennessee. An honest man, with too much faith in human nature, little aptitude for business and intricate detail, he had had large opportunity of becoming acquainted at first hand with much of the work before him. And of that work it has been truly said that "no approximately correct history of civilization can ever be written which does not throw out in bold relief, as one of the great landmarks of political and social progress, the organization and administration of the Freedmen's Bureau."

* * *

THE
CIVIL WAR

Shelby Foote, the author of the monumental history The Civil War, *says that that conflict defined the country. "It is very necessary, if you're going to understand the American character in the twentieth century, to learn about this enormous catastrophe of the mid-nineteenth century." These few pieces tell something of the conflict. Julia Ward Howe (1819–1910) wrote "Battle-Hymn of the Republic" after being touched by the problems of widows of the war. It was first published in* Atlantic Monthly *in February 1862. Union general Ulysses S. Grant (1822—1885), eighteenth president of the United States, wrote his memoirs at the instigation of Mark Twain. He finished them just before his death. Grant memorably described one of the pivotal battles, Shiloh. Our poems are inspired both by some of the great events and figures of the war: The Battle of Gettysburg (1863) and Abraham Lincoln himself but also by the ordinary soldiery.*

Battle-Hymn of the Republic

Julia Ward Howe

Mine eyes have seen the glory of the coming of the Lord:
He is trampling out the vintage where the grapes of wrath are
    stored;
He hath loosed the fateful lightning of his terrible swift sword:
    His truth is marching on.

I have seen Him in the watch-fires of a hundred circling camps;
They have builded Him an altar in the evening dews and damps;
I can read his righteous sentence by the dim and flaring lamps.
    His day is marching on.

I have read a fiery gospel, writ in burnished rows of steel:
"As ye deal with my contemners, so with you my grace shall
    deal;
Let the Hero, born of woman, crush the serpent with his heel,
    Since God is marching on."

He has sounded forth the trumpet that shall never call retreat;
He is sifting out the hearts of men before his judgment-seat:
Oh! be swift, my soul, to answer Him! be jubilant, my feet!
    Our God is marching on.

In the beauty of the lilies Christ was born across the sea,
With a glory in his bosom that transfigures you and me:
As He died to make men holy, let us die to make men free,
    While God is marching on.

FROM

THE PERSONAL MEMOIRS
OF U. S. GRANT

SHILOH

Some two or three miles from Pittsburg landing was a log meeting-house called Shiloh. It stood on the ridge which divides the waters of Snake and Lick creeks, the former emptying into the Tennessee just north of Pittsburg landing, and the latter south. This point was the key to our position and was held by Sherman. His division was at that time wholly raw, no part of it ever having been in an engagement; but I thought this deficiency was more than made up by the superiority of the commander.

* * *

The position of our troops made a continuous line from Lick Creek on the left to Owl Creek, a branch of Snake Creek, on the right, facing nearly south and possibly a little west. The water in all these streams was very high at the time and contributed to protect our flanks. The enemy was compelled, therefore, to attack directly in front. This he did with great vigor, inflicting heavy losses on the National side, but suffering much heavier on his own.

The Confederate assaults were made with such a disregard of losses on their own side that our line of tents soon fell into their hands. The ground on which the battle was fought was undulating, heavily timbered with scattered clearings, the woods giving some protection to the troops on both sides. There was also considerable underbrush. A number of attempts were made by the enemy to turn our right flank, where Sherman was posted, but every effort was repulsed with heavy loss. But the front attack was kept up so vigorously that, to prevent the success of these attempts to get on our flanks, the National troops were compelled, several times, to take positions to the rear nearer Pittsburg landing. When the firing ceased at night the National line was all of a mile in rear of the position it had occupied in the morning.

In one of the backward moves, on the 6th, the division commanded by General Prentiss did not fall back with the others. This left his flanks exposed and enabled the enemy to capture him with about 2,200 of his officers and men. General Badeau gives four o'clock of the 6th as about the time this capture took place. He may be right as to the time, but my recollection is that the hour was later. General Prentiss himself gave the hour as half-past five. I was with him, as I was with each of the division commanders that day, several times, and my recollection is that the last time I was with him was about half-past four, when his division was standing up firmly and the General was as cool as if expecting victory. But no matter whether it was four or later, the story that he and his command were surprised and captured in their camps is without any foundation whatever. If it had been true, as currently reported at the time and yet believed by thousands of people, that Prentiss and his division had been captured in their beds, there would not have been an all-day struggle, with the loss of thousands killed and wounded on the Confederate side.

With the single exception of a few minutes after the capture of Prentiss, a continuous and unbroken line was maintained all day from Snake Creek or its tributaries on the right to Lick Creek or the Tennessee on the left above Pittsburg. There was no hour during the day when there was not heavy firing and generally hard fighting at some point on the line, but seldom at all points at the same time. It was a case of Southern dash against Northern pluck and endurance. Three of the five divisions engaged on Sunday were entirely raw, and many of the men had only received their arms on the way from their States to the field. Many of them had arrived but a day or two before and were hardly able to load their muskets according to the manual. Their officers were equally ignorant of their duties. Under these circumstances it is not astonishing that many of the regiments broke at the first fire. In two cases, as I now remember, colonels led their regiments from the field on first hearing the whistle of the enemy's bullets. In these cases the colonels were constitutional cowards, unfit for any military position; but not so the officers and men led out of danger by them. Better troops never went upon a battle-field than many of these, officers and men, afterwards proved themselves to be, who fled panic-stricken at the first whistle of bullets and shell at Shiloh.

During the whole of Sunday I was continuously engaged in passing from one part of the field to another, giving directions to division commanders. In thus moving along the line, however, I never deemed it important to stay long with Sherman. Although his troops were then under fire for the first time, their commander, by his constant presence with them, inspired a confidence in officers and men that enabled them to render services on that bloody battle-field worthy of the best of veterans. McClernand was next to Sherman, and the hardest fighting was in front of these two divisions. McClernand told me on that day, the 6th, that he profited much by having so able a commander supporting him. A casualty to Sherman that would have taken him from the field that day would have been a sad one for the troops engaged at Shiloh. And how near we came to this! On the 6th Sherman was shot twice, once in the hand, once in the shoulder, the ball cutting his coat and making a slight wound, and a third ball passed through his hat. In addition to this he had several horses shot during the day.

The nature of this battle was such that cavalry could not be used in front; I therefore formed ours into line in rear, to stop stragglers—of whom there were many. When there would be enough of them to make a show, and after they had recovered from their fright, they would be sent to reinforce some part of the line which needed support, without regard to their companies, regiments or brigades.

On one occasion during the day I rode back as far as the river and met General Buell, who had just arrived; I do not remember the hour, but at that time there probably were as many as four or five thousand stragglers lying under cover of the river bluff, panic-stricken, most of whom would have been shot where they lay, without resistance, before they would have taken muskets and marched to the front to protect themselves. This meeting between General Buell and myself was on the dispatch-boat used to run between the landing and Savannah. It was brief, and related specially to his getting his troops over the river. As we left the boat together, Buell's attention was attracted by the men lying under cover of the river bank. I saw him berating them and trying to shame them into joining their regiments. He even threatened them with shells from the gunboats near by. But it was all to no effect. Most of these men afterward proved themselves as gallant as any of those who saved the battle from which they had deserted. I have no doubt that this sight impressed General Buell with the idea that a line of retreat would be a good thing just then. If he had come in by the front instead of through the stragglers in the rear, he would have thought and felt differently. Could he have come through the Confederate rear, he would have witnessed there a scene similar to that at our own. The distant rear of an army engaged in battle is not the best place from which to judge correctly what is going on in front. Later in the war, while occupying the country between the Tennessee and the Mississippi, I learned that the panic in the Confederate lines had not differed much from that within our own. Some of the country people estimated the stragglers from Johnston's army as high as 20,000. Of course this was an exaggeration.

* * *

General Lew. Wallace, with 5,000 effective men, arrived after firing had ceased for the day, and was placed on the right. Thus night came, Wallace came, and the advance of Nelson's division came; but none—unless night—in time to be of material service to the gallant men who saved Shiloh on that first day against large odds. Buell's loss on the 6th of April was two men killed and one wounded, all members of the 36th Indiana infantry. The Army of the Tennessee lost on that day at least 7,000 men. The presence of two or three regiments of Buell's army on the west bank before firing ceased had not the slightest effect in preventing the capture of Pittsburg landing.

So confident was I before firing had ceased on the 6th that the next day would bring victory to our arms if we could only take the initiative, that I visited each division commander in person before any reinforcements had reached the field. I directed them to throw out heavy lines of skirmishers in the morning as soon as they could see, and push them forward until they found the enemy, following with their entire divisions in supporting distance, and to engage the enemy as soon as found. To Sherman I told the story of the assault at Fort Donelson, and said that the same tactics would win at Shiloh. Victory was assured when Wallace arrived, even if there had been no other support. I was glad, however, to see the reinforcements of Buell and credit them with doing all there was for them to do. During the night of the 6th the remainder of Nelson's division, Buell's army, crossed the river and were ready to advance in the morning, forming the left wing. Two other divisions, Crittenden's and McCook's, came up the river from Savannah in the transports and were on the west bank early on the 7th. Buell commanded them in person. My command was thus nearly doubled in numbers and efficiency.

During the night rain fell in torrents and our troops were exposed to the storm without shelter. I made my headquarters under a tree a few hundred yards back from the river bank. My ankle was so much swollen from the fall of my horse the Friday night preceding, and the bruise was so painful, that I could get no rest. The drenching rain would have precluded the possibility of sleep without this additional cause. Some time after midnight, growing restive under the storm and the continuous pain, I moved back to the log-house under the bank. This had been taken as a hospital, and all night wounded men were being brought in, their wounds dressed, a leg or an arm amputated as the case might require, and everything being done to save life or alleviate suffering. The sight was more unendurable than encountering the enemy's fire, and I returned to my tree in the rain.

The advance on the morning of the 7th developed the enemy in the camps occupied by our troops before the battle began, more than a mile back from the most advanced position of the Confederates on the day before.

* * *

In a very short time the battle became general all along the line. This day everything was favorable to the Union side. We had now become the attacking party. The enemy was driven back all day, as we had been the day before, until finally he beat a precipitate retreat. The last point held by him was near the road leading from the landing to

Corinth, on the left of Sherman and right of McClernand. About three o'clock, being near that point and seeing that the enemy was giving way everywhere else, I gathered up a couple of regiments, or parts of regiments, from troops near by, formed them in line of battle and marched them forward, going in front myself to prevent premature or long-range firing. At this point there was a clearing between us and the enemy favorable for charging, although exposed. I knew the enemy were ready to break and only wanted a little encouragement from us to go quickly and join their friends who had started earlier. After marching to within musket-range I stopped and let the troops pass. The command, *Charge*, was given, and was executed with loud cheers and with a run; when the last of the enemy broke.

John Burns of Gettysburg

Bret Harte

Have you heard the story that gossips tell
Of Burns of Gettysburg? No? Ah, well:
Brief is the glory that hero earns,
Briefer the story of poor John Burns:
He was the fellow who won renown,—
The only man who did n't back down
When the rebels rode through his native town;
But held his own in the fight next day,
When all his townsfolk ran away.
That was in July, sixty-three,—
The very day that General Lee,
Flower of Southern chivalry,
Baffled and beaten, backward reeled
From a stubborn Meade and a barren field.

I might tell how, but the day before,
John Burns stood at his cottage door,
Looking down the village street,
Where, in the shade of his peaceful vine,
He heard the low of his gathered kine,
And felt their breath with incense sweet;
Or I might say, when the sunset burned
The old farm gable, he thought it turned
The milk that fell like a babbling flood
Into the milk-pail, red as blood!
Or how he fancied the hum of bees
Were bullets buzzing among the trees.
But all such fanciful thoughts as these
Were strange to a practical man like Burns,
Who minded only his own concerns,
Troubled no more by fancies fine
Than one of his calm-eyed, long-tailed kine,

Quite old-fashioned and matter-of-fact,
Slow to argue, but quick to act.
That was the reason, as some folks say,
He fought so well on that terrible day.

And it was terrible. On the right
Raged for hours the heady fight,
Thundered the battery's double bass,—
Difficult music for men to face;
While on the left—where now the graves
Undulate like the living waves
That all that day unceasing swept
Up to the pits the rebels kept—
Round-shot ploughed the upland glades,
Sown with bullets, reaped with blades;
Shattered fences here and there
Tossed their splinters in the air;
The very trees were stripped and bare;
The barns that once held yellow grain
Were heaped with harvests of the slain;
The cattle bellowed on the plain,
The turkeys screamed with might and main
The brooding barn-fowl left their rest
With strange shells bursting in each nest.

Just where the tide of battle turns,
Erect and lonely, stood old John Burns.
How do you think the man was dressed?
He wore an ancient, long buff vest,
Yellow as saffron,—but his best;
And, buttoned over his manly breast,
Was a bright blue coat with a rolling collar,
And large gilt buttons,—size of a dollar,—
With tails that the country-folk called "swaller."
He wore a broad-brimmed, bell-crowned hat,
White as the locks on which it sat.

Never had such a sight been seen
For forty years on the village green,
Since old John Burns was a country beau,
And went to the "quiltings" long ago.

Close at his elbows all that day,
Veterans of the Peninsula,
Sunburnt and bearded, charged away;
And striplings, downy of lip and chin,—
Clerks that the Home-Guard mustered in,—
Glanced, as they passed, at the hat he wore,
Then at the rifle his right hand bore;
And hailed him, from out their youthful lore,
With scraps of a slangy repertoire:
"How are you, White Hat?" "Put her through!"
"Your head's level!" and "Bully for you!"
Called him "Daddy,"—begged he'd disclose
The name of his tailor who made his clothes,
And what was the value he set on those;
While Burns, unmindful of jeer or scoff,
Stood there picking the rebels off,—
With his long brown rifle, and bell-crowned hat,
And the swallow-tails they were laughing at.

'T was but a moment, for that respect
Which clothes all courage their voices checked;
And something the wildest could understand
Spake in the old man's strong right hand,
And his corded throat, and the lurking frown
Of his eyebrows under his old bell-crown;
Until, as they gazed, there crept an awe
Through the ranks in whispers, and some men
        saw,
In the antique vestments and long white hair,
The Past of the Nation in battle there;
And some of the soldiers since declare
That the gleam of his old white hat afar,

Like the crested plume of the brave Navarre,
That day was their oriflamme of war.

So raged the battle. You know the rest:
How the rebels, beaten and backward pressed,
Broke at the final charge and ran.
At which John Burns—a practical man—
Shouldered his rifle, unbent his brows,
And then went back to his bees and cows.

That is the story of old John Burns;
This is the moral the reader learns:
In fighting the battle, the question's whether
You'll show a hat that's white, or a feather.

THE BLUE AND THE GRAY

Francis Miles Finch

By the flow of the inland river,
   Whence the fleets of iron have fled,
Where the blades of the grave grass quiver,
   Asleep are the ranks of the dead;—
     Under the sod and the dew,
      Waiting the judgment day;—
     Under the one, the Blue;
      Under the other, the Gray.

These in the robings of glory,
   Those in the gloom of defeat,
All with the battle blood gory,
   In the dusk of eternity meet;—
     Under the sod and the dew,
      Waiting the judgment day;—
     Under the laurel, the Blue;
      Under the willow, the Gray.

From the silence of sorrowful hours
   The desolate mourners go,
Lovingly laden with flowers
   Alike for the friend and the foe,—
     Under the sod and the dew,
      Waiting the judgment day;—
     Under the roses, the Blue;
      Under the lilies, the Gray.

So with an equal splendor
   The morning sun rays fall,
With a touch, impartially tender,
   On the blossoms blooming for all;—
     Under the sod and the dew,

Waiting the judgment day;—
'Broidered with gold, the Blue;
Mellowed with gold, the Gray.

So, when the summer calleth,
On forest and field of grain
With an equal murmur falleth
The cooling drip of the rain;—
Under the sod and the dew,
Waiting the judgment day;—
Wet with the rain, the Blue;
Wet with the rain, the Gray.

Sadly, but not with upbraiding,
The generous deed was done;
In the storm of the years that are fading,
No braver battle was won;—
Under the sod and the dew,
Waiting the judgment day;—
Under the blossoms, the Blue;
Under the garlands, the Gray.

No more shall the war cry sever,
Or the winding rivers be red;
They banish our anger forever
When they laurel the graves of our dead!
Under the sod and the dew,
Waiting the judgment day;—
Love and tears for the Blue,
Tears and love for the Gray.

When Johnny Comes Marching Home

Patrick Sarsfield Gilmore

WHEN Johnny comes marching home again,
    Hurrah! hurrah!
We'll give him a hearty welcome then,
    Hurrah! hurrah!
The men will cheer, the boys will shout,
The ladies, they will all turn out,
    And we'll all feel gay,
When Johnny comes marching home.

The old church-bell will peal with joy,
    Hurrah! hurrah!
To welcome home our darling boy,
    Hurrah! hurrah!
The village lads and lasses say,
With roses they will strew the way;
    And we'll all feel gay,
When Johnny comes marching home.

Get ready for the jubilee,
    Hurrah! hurrah!
We'll give the hero three times three,
    Hurrah! hurrah!
The laurel-wreath is ready now
To place upon his loyal brow,
    And we'll all feel gay,
When Johnny comes marching home.

Let love and friendship on that day,
    Hurrah! hurrah!
Their choicest treasures then display,

Hurrah! hurrah!
And let each one perform some part,
To fill with joy the warrior's heart;
And we'll all feel gay,
When Johnny comes marching home.

O Captain! My Captain!

Walt Whitman

O Captain! my Captain! our fearful trip is done,
The ship has weathered every rack, the prize we sought is won,
The port is near, the bells I hear, the people all exulting,
While follow eyes the steady keel, the vessel grim and daring;
    But O heart! heart! heart!
      O the bleeding drops of red,
    Where on the deck my Captain lies,
      Fallen cold and dead.

O Captain! my Captain! rise up and hear the bells;
Rise up—for you the flag is flung—for you the bugle trills,
For you bouquets and ribboned wreaths—for you the shores a-
    crowding,
For you they call, the swaying mass, their eager faces turning;
    Here Captain! dear father!
      This arm beneath your head!
    It is some dream that on the deck
      You've fallen cold and dead.

My Captain does not answer, his lips are pale and still,
My father does not feel my arm, he has no pulse nor will,
The ship is anchored safe and sound, its voyage closed and done,
From fearful trip the victor ship comes in with object won;
    Exult O shores, and ring O bells!
      But I with mournful tread,
    Walk the deck my Captain lies,
      Fallen cold and dead.

THE SOUTH

Together with the Missouri River, the Mississippi is over four thousand miles long and is clearly more than a "Southern" phenomenon. But the state that bears its name is indisputably in the south, so Mark Twain's contribution takes its place here. Life on the Mississippi *was published in 1883, Twain having revisited the river of his youth for a series of articles in 1875 and again in 1882. Mark Twain, born Samuel Langhorne Clemens in 1835, worked from 1857 to 1861 on Mississippi steamboats, eventually as a licensed pilot. Kate Chopin was born Katherine O'Flaherty in St. Louis in 1851, when, a few years after Francis Parkman visited, it was a frontier town of seventy-five thousand. She lived most of her life there, but lived in New Orleans while married to Oscar Chopin, a cotton broker with whom she had five children. After Oscar's sudden death in 1882, Chopin returned to St. Louis and began to write, most notably* The Awakening *(1899). "Beyond the Bayou" comes from the collection* Bayou Folk *(1894).*

FROM

LIFE ON THE MISSISSIPPI

Mark Twain

THE RIVER AND ITS HISTORY

The Mississippi is well worth reading about. It is not a commonplace river, but on the contrary is in all ways remarkable. Considering the Missouri its main branch, it is the longest river in the world—four thousand three hundred miles. It seems safe to say that it is also the crookedest river in the world, since in one part of its journey it uses up one thousand three hundred miles to cover the same ground that the crow would fly over in six hundred and seventy-five. It discharges three times as much water as the St. Lawrence, twenty-five times as much as the Rhine, and three hundred and thirty-eight times as much as the Thames. No other river has so vast a drainage-basin: it draws its water supply from twenty-eight States and Territories; from Delaware, on the Atlantic seaboard, and from all the country between that and Idaho on the Pacific slope—a spread of forty-five degrees of longitude. The Mississippi receives and carries to the Gulf water from fifty-four subordinate rivers that are navigable by steamboats, and from some hundreds that are navigable by flats and keels. The area of its drainage-basin is as great as the combined areas of England, Wales, Scotland, Ireland, France, Spain, Portugal, Germany, Austria, Italy, and Turkey; and almost all this wide region is fertile; the Mississippi valley, proper, is exceptionally so.

It is a remarkable river in this: that instead of widening toward its mouth, it grows narrower; grows narrower and deeper. From the junction of the Ohio to a point half way down to the sea, the width averages a mile in high water: thence to the sea the width steadily diminishes, until, at the "Passes," above the mouth, it is but little over half a mile. At the junction of the Ohio the Mississippi's depth is eighty-seven feet; the depth increases gradually, reaching one hundred and twenty-nine just above the mouth.

The difference in rise and fall is also remarkable—not in the upper, but in the lower river. The rise is tolerably uniform down to Natchez (three hundred and sixty miles above the mouth)—about fifty feet. But at Bayou La Fourche the river rises only twenty-four feet; at New Orleans only fifteen, and just above the mouth only two and one half.

An article in the New Orleans "Times-Democrat," based upon reports of able engineers, states that the river annually empties four hundred and six million tons of mud into the Gulf of Mexico—which brings to mind Captain Marryat's rude name for the Mississippi—"the Great Sewer." This mud, solidified, would make a mass a mile square and two hundred and forty-one feet high.

The mud deposit gradually extends the land—but only gradually; it has extended it not quite a third of a mile in the two hundred years which have elapsed since the river took its place in history. The belief of the scientific people is, that the mouth used to be at Baton Rouge, where the hills cease, and that the two hundred miles of land between there and the Gulf was built by the river. This gives us the age of that piece of country, without any trouble at all—one hundred and twenty thousand years. Yet it is much the youthfulest batch of country that lies around there anywhere.

The Mississippi is remarkable in still another way—its disposition to make prodigious jumps by cutting through narrow necks of land, and thus straightening and shortening itself. More than once it has shortened itself thirty miles at a single jump! These cut-offs have had curious effects: they have thrown several river towns out into the rural districts, and built up sand bars and forests in front of them. The town of Delta used to be three miles below Vicksburg: a recent cut-off has radically changed the position, and Delta is now *two miles above* Vicksburg.

Both of these river towns have been retired to the country by that cut-off. A cut-off plays havoc with boundary lines and jurisdictions: for instance, a man is living in the State of Mississippi to-day, a cut-off occurs to-night, and to-morrow the man finds himself and his land over on the other side of the river, within the boundaries and subject to the laws of the State of Louisiana! Such a thing, happening in the upper river in the old times, could have transferred a slave from Missouri to Illinois and made a free man of him.

The Mississippi does not alter its locality by cut-offs alone: it is always changing its habitat *bodily*—is always moving bodily *sidewise.* At Hard Times, La., the river is two miles west of the region it used to occupy. As a result, the original *site* of that settlement is not now in Louisiana at all, but on the other side of the river, in the State of Mississippi. *Nearly the whole of that one thousand three hundred miles of old Mississippi River which La Salle floated down in his canoes, two hundred years ago, is good solid dry ground now.* The river lies to the right of it, in places, and to the left of it in other places.

Although the Mississippi's mud builds land but slowly, down at the mouth, where the Gulf's billows interfere with its work, it builds fast enough in better protected regions higher up: for instance, Prophet's Island contained one thousand five hundred acres of land thirty years ago; since then the river has added seven hundred acres to it.

But enough of these examples of the mighty stream's eccentricities for the present—I will give a few more of them further along in the book.

Let us drop the Mississippi's physical history, and say a word about its historical history—so to speak. We can glance briefly at its slumbrous first epoch in a couple of short chapters; at its second and wider-awake epoch in a couple more; at its flushest and widest-awake epoch in a good many succeeding chapters; and then talk about its comparatively tranquil present epoch in what shall be left of the book.

The world and the books are so accustomed to use, and over-use, the word "new" in connection with our country, that we early get and permanently retain the impression that there is nothing old about it. We do of course know that there are several comparatively old dates in American history, but the mere figures convey to our minds no just idea, no distinct realization, of the stretch of time which they represent. To say that De Soto, the first white man who ever saw the Mississippi River, saw it in 1542, is a remark which states a fact without interpreting it: it is something like giving the dimensions of a sunset by astronomical measurements, and cataloguing the colors by their scientific names;—as a result, you get the bald fact of the sunset, but you don't see the sunset. It would have been better to paint a picture of it.

The date 1542, standing by itself, means little or nothing to us; but when one groups a few neighboring historical dates and facts around it, he adds perspective and color, and then realizes that this is one of the American dates which is quite respectable for age.

For instance, when the Mississippi was first seen by a white man, less than a quarter of a century had elapsed since Francis I.'s defeat at Pavia; the death of Raphael; the death of Bayard, *sans peur et sans reproche;* the driving out of the Knights-Hospitallers from Rhodes by the Turks; and the placarding of the Ninety-Five Propositions,—the act which began the Reformation. When De Soto took his glimpse of the river, Ignatius Loyola was an obscure name; the order of the Jesuits was not yet a year old; Michael Angelo's paint was not yet dry on the Last Judgment in the Sistine Chapel; Mary Queen of Scots was not yet born, but would be before the year closed. Catherine de Medici was a child; Elizabeth of England was not yet in her teens; Calvin, Benvenuto Cellini, and the Emperor Charles V. were at the top of their fame, and each was manufacturing history after his own peculiar fashion; Margaret of Navarre was writing the "Heptameron" and some religious books,—the first survives, the others are forgotten, wit and indelicacy being sometimes better literature-preservers than holiness; lax court morals and the absurd chivalry business were in full feather, and the joust and the tournament were the frequent pastime of titled fine gentlemen who could fight better than they could spell, while religion was the passion of their ladies, and the classifying their offspring into children of full rank and children by brevet their pastime. In fact, all around, religion was in a peculiarly blooming condition: the Council of Trent was being called; the Spanish Inquisition was roasting, and racking, and burning, with a free hand; elsewhere on the continent the nations were being persuaded to holy living by the sword and fire; in England, Henry VIII. had suppressed the monasteries, burnt Fisher and another bishop or two, and was getting his English reformation and his harem effectively started. When De Soto stood on the banks of the Mississippi, it was still two years before Luther's death; eleven years before the burning of Servetus; thirty years before the St. Bartholomew slaughter; Rabelais was not yet published; "Don Quixote" was not yet written; Shakespeare was not yet born; a hundred long years must still elapse before Englishmen would hear the name of Oliver Cromwell.

Unquestionably the discovery of the Mississippi is a datable fact which considerably mellows and modifies the shiny newness of our country, and gives her a most respectable outside-aspect of rustiness and antiquity.

De Soto merely glimpsed the river, then died and was buried in it by his priests and soldiers. One would expect the priests and the soldiers to multiply the river's dimensions by ten—the Spanish custom of the day—and thus move other adventurers to go at once and explore it. On the contrary, their narratives when they reached home, did not excite that amount of curiosity. The Mississippi was left unvisited by whites during a term of years which seems incredible in our energetic days. One may "sense" the interval to his mind, after a fashion, by dividing it up in this way: After De Soto glimpsed the river, a fraction short of a quarter of a century elapsed, and then Shakespeare was born; lived a trifle more than half a century, then died; and when he had been in his grave considerably more than half a century, the *second* white man saw the Mississippi. In our day we don't allow a hundred and thirty years to elapse between glimpses of a marvel. If somebody should discover a creek in the county next to the one that the North Pole is in, Europe and America would start fifteen costly expeditions thither: one to explore the creek, and the other fourteen to hunt for each other.

For more than a hundred and fifty years there had been white settlements on our Atlantic coasts. These people were in intimate communication with the Indians: in the south the Spaniards were robbing, slaughtering, enslaving and converting them; higher up, the English were trading beads and blankets to them for a consideration, and throwing in civilization and whiskey, "for lagniappe;" and in Canada the French were schooling them in a rudimentary way, missionarying among them, and drawing whole populations of them at a time to

Quebec, and later to Montreal, to buy furs of them. Necessarily, then, these various clusters of whites must have heard of the great river of the far west; and indeed, they did hear of it vaguely,—so vaguely and indefinitely, that its course, proportions, and locality were hardly even guessable. The mere mysteriousness of the matter ought to have fired curiosity and compelled exploration; but this did not occur. Apparently nobody was curious about it; so, for a century and a half the Mississippi remained out of the market and undisturbed. When De Soto found it, he was not hunting for a river, and had no present occasion for one; consequently he did not value it or even take any particular notice of it.

But at last La Salle the Frenchman conceived the idea of seeking out that river and exploring it. It always happens that when a man seizes upon a neglected and important idea, people inflamed with the same notion crop up all around. It happened so in this instance.

Naturally the question suggests itself, Why did these people want the river now when nobody had wanted it in the five preceding generations? Apparently it was because at this late day they thought they had discovered a way to make it useful; for it had come to be believed that the Mississippi emptied into the Gulf of California, and therefore afforded a short cut from Canada to China. Previously the supposition had been that it emptied into the Atlantic, or Sea of Virginia.

BEYOND THE BAYOU

Kate Chopin

The bayou curved like a crescent around the point of land on which La Folle's cabin stood. Between the stream and the hut lay a big abandoned field, where cattle were pastured when the bayou supplied them with water enough. Through the woods that spread back into unknown regions the woman had drawn an imaginary line, and past this circle she never stepped. This was the form of her only mania.

She was now a large, gaunt black woman, past thirty-five. Her real name was Jacqueline, but every one on the plantation called her La Folle, because in childhood she had been frightened literally "out of her senses," and had never wholly regained them.

It was when there had been skirmishing and sharpshooting all day in the woods. Evening was near when P'tit Maître, black with powder and crimson with blood, had staggered into the cabin of Jacqueline's mother, his pursuers close at his heels. The sight had stunned her childish reason.

She dwelt alone in her solitary cabin, for the rest of the quarters had long since been removed beyond her sight and knowledge. She had more physical strength than most men, and made her patch of cotton and corn and tobacco like the best of them. But of the world beyond the bayou she had long known nothing, save what her morbid fancy conceived.

People at Bellissime had grown used to her and her way, and they thought nothing of it. Even when "Old Mis' " died, they did not wonder that La Folle had not crossed the bayou, but had stood upon her side of it, wailing and lamenting.

P'tit Maître was now the owner of Bellissime. He was a middle-aged man, with a family of beautiful daughters about him, and a little son whom La Folle loved as if he had been her own. She called him Chéri, and so did every one else because she did.

None of the girls had ever been to her what Chéri was. They had each and all loved to be with her, and to listen to her wondrous stories of things that always happened "yonda, beyon' de bayou."

But none of them had stroked her black hand quite as Chéri did, nor rested their heads against her knee so confidingly, nor fallen asleep in her arms as he used to do. For Chéri hardly did such things now, since he had become the proud possessor of a gun, and had had his black curls cut off.

That summer—the summer Chéri gave La Folle two black curls tied with a knot of red ribbon—the water ran so low in the bayou that even the little children at Bellissime were able to cross it on foot, and the cattle were sent to pasture down by the river. La Folle was sorry when they were gone, for she loved these dumb companions well, and liked to feel that they were there, and to hear them browsing by night up to her own inclosure.

It was Saturday afternoon, when the fields were deserted. The men had flocked to a neighboring village to do their week's trading, and the women were occupied with household affairs,—La Folle as well as the others. It was then she mended and washed her handful of clothes, scoured her house, and did her baking.

In this last employment she never forgot Chéri. Today she had fashioned croquignoles of the most fantastic and alluring shapes for him. So when she saw the boy come trudging across the old field with his gleaming little new rifle on his shoulder, she called out gayly to him, "Chéri! Chéri!"

But Chéri did not need the summons, for he was coming straight to her. His pockets all bulged out with almonds and raisins and an orange that he had secured for her from the very fine dinner which had been given that day up at his father's house.

He was a sunny-faced youngster of ten. When he had emptied his pockets, La Folle patted his round red cheek, wiped his soiled hands on her apron, and smoothed his hair. Then she watched him as, with his cakes in his hand, he crossed her strip of cotton back of the cabin, and disappeared into the wood.

He had boasted of the things he was going to do with his gun out there.

"You think they got plenty deer in the wood, La Folle?" he had inquired, with the calculating air of an experienced hunter.

"Non, non!" the woman laughed. "Don't you look fo' no deer, Chéri. Dat's too big. But you bring La Folle one good fat squirrel fo' her dinner tomorrow, an' she goin' be satisfi'."

"One squirrel ain't a bite. I'll bring you mo' 'an one, La Folle," he had boasted pompously as he went away.

When the woman, an hour later, heard the report of the boy's rifle close to the wood's edge, she would have thought nothing of it if a sharp cry of distress had not followed the sound.

She withdrew her arms from the tub of suds in which they had been plunged, dried them upon her apron, and as quickly as her trembling limbs would bear her, hurried to the spot whence the ominous report had come.

It was as she feared. There she found Chéri stretched upon the ground, with his rifle beside him. He moaned piteously:—

"I'm dead, La Folle! I'm dead! I'm gone!"

"Non, non!" she exclaimed resolutely, as she knelt beside him. "Put you' arm 'roun' La Folle's nake, Chéri. Dat's nuttin'; dat goin' be nuttin'." She lifted him in her powerful arms.

Chéri had carried his gun muzzle-downward. He had stumbled— he did not know how. He only knew that he had a ball lodged somewhere in his leg, and he thought that his end was at hand. Now, with his head upon the woman's shoulder, he moaned and wept with pain and fright.

"Oh, La Folle! La Folle! it hurt so bad! I can' stan' it, La Folle!"

"Don't cry, *mon bébé, mon Chéri!*" the woman spoke soothingly as she covered the ground with long strides. "La Folle goin' mine you; Doctor Bonfils goin' come make *mon Chéri* well agin."

She had reached the abandoned field. As she crossed it with her precious burden, she looked constantly and restlessly from side to side. A terrible fear was upon her,—the fear of the world beyond the bayou, the morbid and insane dread she had been under since childhood.

When she was at the bayou's edge she stood there, and shouted for help as if a life depended upon it:—

"Oh, P'tit Maître! P'tit Maître! Venez donc! Au secours! Au secours!"

No voice responded. Chéri's hot tears were scalding her neck. She called for each and every one upon the place, and still no answer came.

She shouted, she wailed; but whether her voice remained unheard or unheeded, no reply came to her frenzied cries. And all the while Chéri moaned and wept and entreated to be taken home to his mother.

La Folle gave a last despairing look around her. Extreme terror was upon her. She clasped the child close against her breast, where he could feel her heart beat like a muffled hammer. Then shutting her eyes, she ran suddenly down the shallow bank of the bayou, and never stopped till she had climbed the opposite shore.

She stood there quivering an instant as she opened her eyes. Then she plunged into the footpath through the trees.

She spoke no more to Chéri, but muttered constantly, "Bon Dieu, ayez pitié La Folle! Bon Dieu, ayez pitié moi!"

Instinct seemed to guide her. When the pathway spread clear and smooth enough before her, she again closed her eyes tightly against the sight of that unknown and terrifying world.

A child, playing in some weeds, caught sight of her as she neared the quarters. The little one uttered a cry of dismay.

"La Folle!" she screamed, in her piercing treble. "La Folle done cross de bayer!"

Quickly the cry passed down the line of cabins.

"Yonda, La Folle done cross de bayou!"

Children, old men, old women, young ones with infants in their arms, flocked to doors and windows to see this awe-inspiring spectacle. Most of them shuddered with superstitious dread of what it might portend. "She totin' Chéri!" some of them shouted.

Some of the more daring gathered about her, and followed at her heels, only to fall back with new terror when she turned her distorted face upon them. Her eyes were bloodshot and the saliva had gathered in a white foam on her black lips.

Some one had run ahead of her to where P'tit Maître sat with his family and guests upon the gallery.

"P'tit Maître! La Folle done cross de bayou! Look her! Look her yonda totin' Chéri!" This startling intimation was the first which they had of the woman's approach.

She was now near at hand. She walked with long strides. Her eyes were fixed desperately before her, and she breathed heavily, as a tired ox.

At the foot of the stairway, which she could not have mounted, she laid the boy in his father's arms. Then the world that had looked red to La Folle suddenly turned black—like that day she had seen powder and blood.

She reeled for an instant. Before a sustaining arm could reach her, she fell heavily to the ground.

When La Folle regained consciousness, she was at home again, in her own cabin and upon her own bed. The moon rays, streaming in through the open door and windows, gave what light was needed to the old black mammy who stood at the table concocting a tisane of fragrant herbs. It was very late.

Others who had come, and found that the stupor clung to her, had gone again. P'tit Maître had been there, and with him Doctor Bonfils, who said that La Folle might die.

But death had passed her by. The voice was very clear and steady with which she spoke to Tante Lizette, brewing her tisane there in a corner.

"Ef you will give me one good drink tisane, Tante Lizette, I b'lieve I'm goin' sleep, me."

And she did sleep; so soundly, so healthfully, that old Lizette without compunction stole softly away, to creep back through the moonlit fields to her own cabin in the new quarters.

The first touch of the cool gray morning awoke La Folle. She arose, calmly, as if no tempest had shaken and threatened her existence but yesterday.

She donned her new blue cottonade and white apron, for she remembered that this was Sunday. When she had made for herself a cup of strong black coffee, and drunk it with relish, she quitted the cabin and walked across the old familiar field to the bayou's edge again.

She did not stop there as she had always done before, but crossed with a long, steady stride as if she had done this all her life.

When she had made her way through the brush and scrub cotton-wood trees that lined the opposite bank, she found herself upon the border of a field where the white, bursting cotton, with the dew upon it, gleamed for acres and acres like frosted silver in the early dawn.

La Folle drew a long, deep breath as she gazed across the country. She walked slowly and uncertainly, like one who hardly knows how, looking about her as she went.

The cabins, that yesterday had sent a clamor of voices to pursue her, were quiet now. No one was yet astir at Bellissime. Only the birds that darted here and there from hedges were awake, and singing their matins.

When La Folle came to the broad stretch of velvety lawn that surrounded the house, she moved slowly and with delight over the springy turf, that was delicious beneath her tread.

She stopped to find whence came those perfumes that were assailing her senses with memories from a time far gone.

There they were, stealing up to her from the thousand blue violets that peeped out from green, luxuriant beds. There they were, showering down from the big waxen bells of the magnolias far above her head, and from the jessamine clumps around her.

There were roses, too, without number. To right and left palms spread in broad and graceful curves. It all looked like enchantment beneath the sparkling sheen of dew.

When La Folle had slowly and cautiously mounted the many steps that led up to the veranda, she turned to look back at the perilous ascent she had made. Then she caught sight of the river, bending like a silver bow at the foot of Bellissime. Exultation possessed her soul.

La Folle rapped softly upon a door near at hand. Chéri's mother soon cautiously opened it. Quickly and cleverly she dissembled the astonishment she felt at seeing La Folle.

"Ah, La Folle! Is it you, so early?"

"*Oui,* madame. I come ax how my po' li'le Chéri to, 's mo'nin'."

"He is feeling easier, thank you, La Folle. Dr. Bonfils says it will be nothing serious. He's sleeping now. Will you come back when he awakes?"

"*Non*, madame. I'm goin' wait yair tell Chéri wake up." La Folle seated herself upon the topmost step of the veranda.

A look of wonder and deep content crept into her face as she watched for the first time the sun rise upon the new, the beautiful world beyond the bayou.

THE WEST

Mark Twain's famous jumping frog saw the light of day in 1865 when Twain was living in San Francisco. It helped to establish his name as a humorist of note. "My First Meeting with Wild Bill" was published in Harper's New Monthly Magazine *in February 1867. Bret Harte (1836–1902) was instrumental in popularizing the short story in America. In the 1870s, after the fabulous success of his story "The Luck of Roaring Camp," William Dean Howells, an editor at* Atlantic Monthly, *made him America's best-paid writer. As Harte powerfully evoked the violent life of the gold-mining camps, Billy the Kid lived the life, his six-year rampage ended by Pat Garrett in 1881 when Billy was twenty-one. The account is taken from* The History of Billy the Kid *by Charles A. Siringo. "The Ballad of Jesse James" paints a more romantic vision of the life of the frontier bandit. Together, these extracts give some picture of the lawlessness and violence of the new territories.*

THE CELEBRATED JUMPING FROG
OF CALAVERAS COUNTY

Mark Twain

In compliance with the request of a friend of mine, who wrote me from the East, I called on good-natured, garrulous old Simon Wheeler, and inquired after my friend's friend, Leonidas W. Smiley, as requested to do, and I hereunto append the result. I have a lurking suspicion that *Leonidas W.* Smiley is a myth; that my friend never knew such a personage; and that he only conjectured that if I asked old Wheeler about him, it would remind him of his infamous *Jim* Smiley, and he would go to work and bore me to death with some exasperating reminiscence of him as long and as tedious as it should be useless to me. If that was the design, it succeeded.

I found Simon Wheeler dozing comfortably by the bar-room stove of the dilapidated tavern in the decayed mining camp of Angel's, and I noticed that he was fat and bald-headed, and had an expression of winning gentleness and simplicity upon his tranquil countenance. He roused up, and gave me good day. I told him that a friend of mine had commissioned me to make some inquiries about a cherished companion of his boyhood named *Leonidas W.* Smiley—*Rev. Leonidas W.* Smiley, a young minister of the Gospel, who he had heard was at one time a resident of Angel's Camp. I added that if Mr. Wheeler could tell me anything about this Rev. Leonidas W. Smiley, I would feel under many obligations to him.

Simon Wheeler backed me into a corner and blockaded me there with his chair, and then sat down and reeled off the monotonous narrative which follows this paragraph. He never smiled, he never frowned, he never changed his voice from the gentle-flowing key to which he tuned his initial sentence, he never betrayed the slightest suspicion of enthusiasm; but all through the interminable narrative there ran a vein of impressive earnestness and sincerity, which showed me plainly that, so far from his imagining that there was anything ridiculous or funny about his story, he regarded it as a really important matter, and admired its two heroes as men of transcendent genius in *finesse*. I let him go on in his own way, and never interrupted him once.

"Rev. Leonidas W. H'm, Reverend Le—well, there was a feller here once by the name of *Jim* Smiley, in the winter of '49—or maybe it was the spring of '50—I don't recollect exactly, somehow, though what makes me think it was one or the other is because I remember the big flume warn't finished when he first come to camp; but anyway, he was the curiousest man about always betting on anything that turned up you ever see, if he could get anybody to bet on the other side; and if he couldn't he'd change sides. Any way that suited the other man would suit *him*—any way just so's he got a bet, *he* was satisfied. But still he was lucky, uncommon lucky; he most always come out winner. He was always ready and laying for a chance; there couldn't be no solit'ry thing mentioned but that feller'd offer to bet on it, and take ary side you please, as I was just telling you. If there was a horse-race, you'd find him flush or you'd find him busted at the end of it; if there was a dog-fight, he'd bet on it; if there was a cat-fight, he'd bet on it; if there was a chicken-fight, he'd bet on it; why, if there was two birds setting on a fence, he would bet you which one would fly first; or if there was a camp-meeting, he would be there reg'lar to bet on Parson Walker, which he judged to be the best exhorter about here, and so he was too, and a good man. If he even see a straddle-bug start to go anywheres, he would bet you how long it would take him to get to—to wherever he was going to, and if you took him up, he would foller that straddle-bug to Mexico but what he would find out where he was bound for and how long he was on the road. Lots of the boys here has seen that Smiley, and can tell you about him. Why, it never made no difference to *him*—he'd bet on *any* thing—the dangdest feller. Parson Walker's wife laid very sick once, for a good while, and it seemed as if they warn't going to save her; but one morning he come in, and Smiley up and asked him how she was, and he said she was considerable better— thank the Lord for his inf'nite mercy—and coming on so smart that with the blessing of Prov'dence she'd get well yet; and Smiley, before he thought, says, 'Well, I'll resk two-and-a-half she don't anyway.'

"Thish-yer Smiley had a mare—the boys called her the fifteen-minute nag, but that was only in fun, you know, because of course she was faster than that—and he used to win money on that horse, for all she was so slow and always had the asthma, or the distemper, or the consumption, or something of that kind. They used to give her two or three hundred yards' start, and then pass her under way; but always at the fag end of the race she'd get excited and desperate like, and come cavorting and straddling up, and scattering her legs around limber, sometimes in the air, and sometimes out to one side among the fences, and kicking up m-o-r-e dust and raising m-o-r-e racket with her coughing and sneezing and blowing her nose—and *always* fetch up at the stand just about a neck ahead, as near as you could cipher it down.

"And he had a little small bull-pup, that to look at him you'd think he warn't worth a cent but to set around and look ornery and lay for a chance to steal something. But as soon as money was up on him he was a different dog; his under-jaw'd begin to stick out like the fo'castle of a steamboat, and his teeth would uncover and shine like the furnaces. And a dog might tackle him and bully-rag him, and bite him, and throw him over his shoulder two or three times, and Andrew Jackson—which was the name of the pup—Andrew Jackson would never let on but what *he* was satisfied, and hadn't expected nothing else—and the bets being doubled and doubled on the other side all the time, till the money was all up; and then all of a sudden he would grab that other dog jest by the j'int of his hind leg and freeze to it—not chaw, you understand, but only just grip and hang on till they throwed up the sponge, if it was a year. Smiley always come out winner on that pup, till he harnessed a dog once that didn't have no hind legs, because they'd been sawed off in a circular saw, and when the thing had gone along far enough, and the money was all up, and he come to make a snatch for his pet holt, he see in a minute how he'd been imposed on, and how the other dog had him in the door, so to speak, and he 'peared surprised, and then he looked sorter discouraged-like, and didn't try no more to win the fight, and so he got shucked out bad. He give Smiley a look, as much as to say his heart was broke, and it was *his* fault, for putting up a dog that hadn't no hind legs for him to take holt of, which was his main dependence in a fight, and then he limped off a piece and laid down and died. It was a good pup, was that Andrew Jackson, and would have made a name for hisself if he'd lived, for the stuff was in him and he had genius—I know it, because he hadn't no opportunities to speak of, and it don't stand to reason that a dog could make such a fight as he could under them circumstances if he hadn't no talent. It always makes me feel sorry when I think of that last fight of his'n, and the way it turned out.

"Well, thish-yer Smiley had rat-tarriers, and chicken cocks, and tom-cats and all them kind of things, till you couldn't rest, and you couldn't fetch nothing for him to bet on but he'd match you. He ketched a frog one day, and took him home, and said he cal'lated to educate him; and so he never done nothing for three months but set in his back yard and learn that frog to jump. And you bet you he *did* learn him, too. He'd give him a little punch behind, and the next minute you'd see that frog whirling in the air like a doughnut—see him turn one summerset, or maybe a couple, if he got a good start, and come down flat-footed and all right, like a cat. He got him up so in the matter of ketching flies, and kep' him in practice so constant, that he'd nail a fly every time as fur as he could see him. Smiley said all a frog wanted was education, and he could do 'most anything—and I believe him. Why, I've seen him set Dan'l Webster down here on this floor—Dan'l Webster was the name of the frog—and sing out, 'Flies, Dan'l, flies!' and quicker'n you could wink he'd spring straight up and snake a fly off'n the counter there, and flop down on the floor ag'in as solid as a gob of mud, and fall to scratching the side of his head with his hind foot as indifferent as if he hadn't no idea he'd been doin' any more'n any frog might do. You never see a frog so modest and straightfor'ard as he was, for all he was so gifted. And when it come to fair and square jumping on a dead level, he could get over more ground at one straddle than any animal of his breed you ever see. Jumping on a dead level was his strong suit, you understand; and when it come to that, Smiley would ante up money on him as long as he had a red. Smiley was monstrous proud of his frog, and well he might be, for fellers that had traveled and been everywheres all said he laid over any frog that ever *they* see.

"Well, Smiley kep' the beast in a little lattice box, and he used to fetch him down-town sometimes and lay for a bet. One day a feller— a stranger in the camp, he was—come acrost him with his box, and says:

" 'What might it be that you've got in the box?'

"And Smiley says, sorter indifferent-like, 'It might be a parrot, or it might be a canary, maybe, but it ain't—it's only just a frog.'

"And the feller took it, and looked at it careful, and turned it round this way and that, and says, 'H'm—so 'tis. Well, what's *he* good for?'

" 'Well,' Smiley says, easy and careless, 'he's good enough for *one* thing, I should judge—he can outjump any frog in Calaveras County.'

"The feller took the box again, and took another long, particular look, and give it back to Smiley, and says, very deliberate, 'Well,' he says, 'I don't see no p'ints about that frog that's any better'n any other frog.'

" 'Maybe you don't,' Smiley says. 'Maybe you understand frogs and maybe you don't understand 'em; maybe you've had experience, and maybe you ain't only a amature, as it were. Anyways, I've got *my* opinion, and I'll resk forty dollars that he can outjump any frog in Calaveras County.'

"And the feller studied a minute, and then says, kinder sad-like, 'Well, I'm only a stranger here, and I ain't got no frog; but if I had a frog, I'd bet you.'

"And then Smiley says, 'That's all right—that's all right—if you'll hold my box a minute, I'll go and get you a frog.' And so the feller took the box, and put up his forty dollars along with Smiley's, and set down to wait.

"So he set there a good while thinking and thinking to himself, and then he got the frog out and prized his mouth open and took a teaspoon and filled him full of quail-shot—filled him pretty near up to his chin—and set him on the floor. Smiley he went to the swamp and slopped around in the mud for a long time, and finally he ketched a frog, and fetched him in, and give him to this feller, and says:

" 'Now, if you're ready, set him alongside of Dan'l, with his fore paws just even with Dan'l's, and I'll give the word.' Then he says, 'One—two—three—*git!*' and him and the feller touched up the frogs from behind, and the new frog hopped off lively, but Dan'l give a heave, and hysted up his shoulders—so—like a Frenchman, but it warn't no use—he couldn't budge; he was planted as solid as a church, and he couldn't no more stir than if he was anchored out. Smiley was a good deal surprised, and he was disgusted too, but he didn't have no idea what the matter was, of course.

"The feller took the money and started away; and when he was going out at the door, he sorter jerked his thumb over his shoulder—so—at Dan'l, and says again, very deliberate, 'Well,' he says, '*I* don't see no p'ints about that frog that's any better'n any other frog.'

"Smiley he stood scratching his head and looking down at Dan'l a long time, and at last he says, 'I do wonder what in the nation that frog throw'd off for—I wonder if there ain't something the matter with him—he 'pears to look mighty baggy, somehow.' And he ketched Dan'l by the nap of the neck, and hefted him, and says, 'Why blame my cats if he don't weigh five pound!' and turned him upside down and he belched out a double handful of shot. And then he see how it was, and he was the maddest man—he set the frog down and took out after that feller, but he never ketched him. And—"

[Here Simon Wheeler heard his name called from the front yard, and got up to see what was wanted.] And turning to me as he moved away, he said: "Just set where you are, stranger, and rest easy—I ain't going to be gone a second."

But, by your leave, I did not think that a continuation of the history of the enterprising vagabond *Jim* Smiley would be likely to afford me much information concerning the Rev. *Leonidas W.* Smiley, and so I started away.

At the door I met the sociable Wheeler returning, and he button-holed me and recommenced.

"Well, thish-yer Smiley had a yaller one-eyed cow that didn't have no tail, only just a short stump like a bannanner, and—"

However, lacking both time and inclination, I did not wait to hear about the afflicted cow, but took my leave.

My First Meeting with Wild Bill

George Ward Nichols

Several months after the ending of the civil war I visited the city of Springfield in Southwest Missouri. Springfield is not a burgh of extensive dimensions, yet it is the largest in that part of the State, and all roads lead to it—which is one reason why it was the *point d'appui*, as well as the base of operations for all military movements during the war.

On a warm summer day I sat watching from the shadow of a broad awning the coming and going of the strange, half-civilized people who, from all the country round, make this a place for barter and trade. Men and women dressed in queer costumes; men with coats and trowsers made of skin, but so thickly covered with dirt and grease as to have defied the identity of the animal when walking in the flesh. Others wore homespun gear, which oftentimes appeared to have seen lengthy service. Many of those people were mounted on horse-back or mule-back, while others urged forward the unwilling cattle attached to creaking, heavily-laden wagons, their drivers snapping their long whips with a report like that of a pistol-shot.

"This yere is Wild Bill, Colonel," said Captain Honesty, an army officer, addressing me. He continued:

"How are yer, Bill? This yere is Colonel N——, who wants ter know yer."

Let me at once describe the personal appearance of the famous Scout of the Plains, William Hitchcock [*sic*], called "Wild Bill," who now advanced toward me, fixing his clear gray eyes on mine in a quick, interrogative way, as if to take "my measure."

The result seemed favorable, for he held forth a small, muscular hand in a frank, open manner. As I looked at him I thought his the handsomest *physique* I had ever seen. In its exquisite manly proportions it recalled the antique. It was a figure Ward would delight to model as a companion to his "Indian."

Bill stood six feet and an inch in his bright yellow moccasins. A deerskin shirt, or frock it might be called, hung jauntily over his shoulders, and revealed a chest whose breadth and depth were remarkable. These lungs had had growth in some twenty years of the free air of the Rocky Mountains. His small, round waist was girthed by a belt which held two of Colt's navy revolvers. His legs sloped gradually from the compact thigh to the feet, which were small, and turned inward as he walked. There was a singular grace and dignity of carriage about that figure which would have called your attention meet it where you would. The head which crowned it was now covered by a large sombrero, underneath which there shone out a quiet, manly face; so gentle is its expression as he greets you as utterly to belie the history of its owner, yet it is not a face to be trifled with. The lips thin and sensitive, the jaw not too square, the cheek bones slightly prominent, a mass of fine dark hair falls below the neck to the shoulders. The eyes, now that you are in friendly intercourse, are as gentle as a woman's. In truth, the woman nature seems prominent throughout, and you would not believe that you were looking into eyes that have pointed the way to death to hundreds of men. Yes, Wild Bill with his own hands has killed hundreds of men. Of that I have not a doubt. "He shoots to kill," as they say on the border.

In vain did I examine the scout's face for some evidence of murderous propensity. It was a gentle face, and singular only in the sharp angle of the eye, and without any physiognomical reason for the opinion, I have thought his wonderful accuracy of aim was indicated by this peculiarity. He told me, however, to use his own words:

"I allers shoot well; but I come ter be perfeck in the mountains by shootin at a dime for a mark, at bets of half a dollar a shot. And then until the war I never drank liquor nor smoked," he continued, with a melancholy expression; "war is demoralizing, it is."

Captain Honesty was right. I was very curious to see "Wild Bill, the Scout," who, a few days before my arrival in Springfield, in a duel at noonday in the public square, at fifty paces, had sent one of Colt's pistol-balls through the heart of a returned Confederate soldier.

Whenever I had met an officer or soldier who had served in the Southwest I heard of Wild Bill and his exploits, until these stories became so frequent and of such an extraordinary character as quite to outstrip personal knowledge of adventure by camp and field; and the hero of those strange tales took shape in my mind as did Jack the Giant Killer or Sinbad the Sailor in childhood days. As then, I now had the most implicit faith in the existence of the individual; but how one man could accomplish such prodigies of strength and feats of daring was a continued wonder.

In front of the shops which lined both sides of the main business street, and about the public square, were groups of men lolling against posts, lying upon the wooden sidewalks, or sitting in chairs. These men were temporary or permanent denizens of the city, and were lazily occupied in doing nothing. The most marked characteristic of the inhabitants seemed to be an indisposition to move, and their highest ambition to let their hair and beards grow.

Here and there upon the street the appearance of the army blue betokened the presence of a returned Union soldier, and the jaunty, confident air with which they carried themselves was all the more striking in its contrast with the indolence which appeared to belong to the place. The only indication of action was the inevitable revolver which everybody, excepting, perhaps, the women, wore about their persons. When people moved in this lazy city they did so slowly and without method. No one seemed in haste. A huge hog wallowed in luxurious ease in a nice bed of mud on the other side of the way, giving vent to gentle grunts of satisfaction. On the platform at my feet lay a large wolf-dog literally asleep with one eye open. He, too, seemed contented to let the world wag idly on.

The loose, lazy spirit of the occasion finally took possession of me, and I sat and gazed and smoked, and it is possible that I might have fallen into a Rip Van Winkle sleep to have been aroused ten years hence by the cry, "Passengers for the flying machine to New York, all aboard!" when I and the drowsing city were roused into life by the clatter and crash of the hoofs of a horse which dashed furiously across the square and down the street. The rider sat perfectly erect, yet following with a grace of motion, seen only in the horsemen of the plains, the rise and fall of the galloping steed. There was only a moment to observe this, for they halted suddenly, while the rider springing to the ground approached the party which the noise had gathered near me.

TENNESSEE'S PARTNER

Bret Harte

I do not think that we ever knew his real name. Our ignorance of it certainly never gave us any social inconvenience, for at Sandy Bar in 1854 most men were christened anew. Sometimes these appellatives were derived from some distinctiveness of dress, as in the case of "Dungaree Jack"; or from some peculiarity of habit, as shown in "Saleratus Bill," so called from an undue proportion of that chemical in his daily bread; or from some unlucky slip, as exhibited in "The Iron Pirate," a mild, inoffensive man, who earned that baleful title by his unfortunate mispronunciation of the term "iron pyrites." Perhaps this may have been the beginning of a rude heraldry; but I am constrained to think that it was because a man's real name in that day rested solely upon his own unsupported statement. "Call yourself Clifford, do you?" said Boston, addressing a timid newcomer with infinite scorn; "hell is full of such Cliffords!" He then introduced the unfortunate man, whose name happened to be really Clifford, as "Jay-bird Charley"—an unhallowed inspiration of the moment that clung to him ever after.

But to return to Tennessee's Partner, whom we never knew by any other than this relative title. That he had ever existed as a separate and distinct individuality we only learned later. It seems that in 1853 he left Poker Flat to go to San Francisco, ostensibly to procure a wife. He never got any farther than Stockton. At that place he was attracted by a young person who waited upon the table at the hotel where he took his meals. One morning he said something to her which caused her to smile not unkindly, to somewhat coquettishly break a plate of toast over his upturned, serious, simple face, and to retreat to the kitchen. He followed her, and emerged a few moments later, covered with more toast and victory. That day week they were married by a justice of the peace, and returned to Poker Flat. I am aware that something more might be made of this episode, but I prefer to tell it as it was current at Sandy Bar—in the gulches and barrooms—where all sentiment was modified by a strong sense of humor.

Of their married felicity but little is known, perhaps for the reason that Tennessee, then living with his partner, one day took occasion to say something to the bride on his own account, at which it is said, she smiled not unkindly and chastely retreated—this time as far as Marysville, where Tennessee followed her, and where they went to housekeeping without the aid of a justice of the peace. Tennessee's Partner took the loss of his wife simply and seriously, as was his fashion. But to everybody's surprise, when Tennessee one day returned from Marysville, without his partner's wife—she having smiled and retreated with somebody else—Tennessee's Partner was the first man to shake his hand and greet him with affection. The boys who had gathered in the cañon to see the shooting were naturally indignant. Their indignation might have found vent in sarcasm but for a certain look in Tennessee's Partner's eye that indicated a lack of humorous appreciation. In fact, he was a grave man, with a steady application to practical detail which was unpleasant in a difficulty.

Meanwhile a popular feeling against Tennessee had grown up on the Bar. He was known to be a gambler; he was suspected to be a thief. In these suspicions Tennessee's Partner was equally compromised; his continued intimacy with Tennessee after the affair above quoted could only be accounted for on the hypothesis of a copartnership of crime. At last Tennessee's guilt became flagrant. One day he overtook a stranger on his way to Red Dog. The stranger afterward related that Tennessee beguiled the time with interesting anecdote and reminiscence, but illogically concluded the interview in the following words: "And now, young man, I'll trouble you for your knife, your pistols, and your money. You see your weppings might get you into trouble at Red Dog, and your money's a temptation to the evilly disposed. I think you said your address was San Francisco. I shall endeavor to call." It may be stated here that Tennessee had a fine flow of humor, which no business preoccupation could wholly subdue.

This exploit was his last. Red Dog and Sandy Bar made common cause against the highwayman. Tennessee was hunted in very much the same fashion as his prototype, the grizzly. As the toils closed around him, he made a desperate dash through the Bar, emptying his revolver at the crowd before the Arcade Saloon, and so on up Grizzly Cañon; but at its farther extremity he was stopped by a small man on a gray horse. The men looked at each other a moment in silence. Both were fearless, both self-possessed and independent; and both types of a civilization that in the seventeenth century would have been called heroic, but in the nineteenth simply "reckless."

"What have you got there?—I call," said Tennessee, quietly.

"Two bowers and an ace," said the stranger, as quietly, showing two revolvers and a bowie knife.

"That takes me," returned Tennessee; and, with this gambler's epigram, he threw away his useless pistol, and rode back with his captor.

It was a warm night. The cool breeze which usually sprang up with the going down of the sun behind the chaparral-crested mountain was that evening withheld from Sandy Bar. The little cañon was stifling with heated resinous odors, and the decaying driftwood on the Bar sent forth faint, sickening exhalations. The feverishness of day and its fierce passions still filled the camp. Lights moved restlessly along the bank of the river, striking no answering reflection from its tawny current. Against the blackness of the pines the windows of the old loft above the express office stood out staringly bright; and through their curtainless panes the loungers below could see the forms of those who were even then deciding the fate of Tennessee. And above all this, etched on the dark firmament, rose the Sierra, remote and passionless, crowned with remoter passionless stars.

The trial of Tennessee was conducted as fairly as was consistent with a judge and jury who felt themselves to some extent obliged to justify, in their verdict, the previous irregularities of arrest and indictment. The law of Sandy Bar was implacable, but not vengeful. The excitement and personal feeling of the chase were over; with Tennessee safe in their hands, they were ready to listen patiently to any defense, which they were already satisfied was insufficient. There being no doubt in their own minds, they were willing to give the prisoner the benefit of any that might exist. Secure in the hypothesis that he ought to be hanged on general principles, they indulged him with more latitude of defense than his reckless hardihood seemed to ask. The judge appeared to be more anxious than the prisoner, who, otherwise unconcerned, evidently took a grim pleasure in the responsibility he had created. "I don't take any hand in this yer game," had been his invariable, but good-humored reply to all questions. The judge—who was also his captor—for a moment vaguely regretted that he had not shot him "on sight" that morning, but presently dismissed this human weakness as unworthy of the judicial mind. Nevertheless, when there was a tap at the door, and it was said that Tennessee's Partner was there on behalf of the prisoner, he was admitted at once without question. Perhaps the younger members of the jury, to whom the proceedings were becoming irksomely thoughtful, hailed him as a relief.

For he was not, certainly, an imposing figure. Short and stout, with a square face, sunburned into a preternatural redness, clad in a loose duck "jumper" and trousers streaked and splashed with red soil, his aspect under any circumstances would have been quaint, and was now even ridiculous. As he stooped to deposit at his feet a heavy carpetbag he was carrying, it became obvious, from partially developed legends and inscriptions, that the material with which his trousers had been patched had been originally intended for a less ambitious covering. Yet he advanced with great gravity, and after having shaken the hand of each person in the room with labored cordiality, he wiped his serious perplexed face on a red bandana handkerchief, a shade lighter than his complexion, laid his powerful hand upon the table to steady himself, and thus addressed the judge:

"I was passin' by," he began, by way of apology, "and I thought I'd just step in and see how things was gittin' on with Tennessee thar—my pardner. It's a hot night. I disremember any sich weather before on the Bar."

He paused a moment, but nobody volunteering any other meteorological recollection, he again had recourse to his pocket handkerchief, and for some moments mopped his face diligently.

"Have you anything to say on behalf of the prisoner?" said the judge finally.

"Thet's it," said Tennessee's Partner, in a tone of relief. "I come yar as Tennessee's pardner—knowing him nigh on four year, off and on, wet and dry, in luck and out o' luck. His ways ain't aller my ways, but thar ain't any p'ints in that young man, thar ain't any liveliness as he's been up to, as I don't know. And you sez to me, sez you—confidential-like, and between man and man—sez you, 'Do you know anything in his behalf?' and I sez to you, sez I—confidential-like, as between man and man—'What should a man know of his pardner?' "

"Is this all you have to say?" asked the judge impatiently, feeling, perhaps, that a dangerous sympathy of humor was beginning to humanize the court.

"Thet's so," continued Tennessee's Partner. "It ain't for me to say anything agin' him. And now, what's the case? Here's Tennessee wants money, wants it bad, and doesn't like to ask it of his old pardner. Well, what does Tennessee do? He lays for a stranger, and he fetches that stranger; and you lays for *him,* and you fetches *him;* and the honors is easy. And I put it to you, bein' a fa'r-minded man, and to you, gentlemen all, as fa'r-minded men, ef this isn't so."

"Prisoner," said the judge, interrupting, "have you any questions to ask this man?"

"No! no!" continued Tennessee's Partner, hastily. "I play this yer hand alone. To come down to the bedrock, it's just this: Tennessee, thar, has played it pretty rough and expensive-like on a stranger, and on this yer camp. And now, what's the fair thing? Some would say more, some would say less. Here's seventeen hundred dollars in coarse gold and a watch,—it's about all my pile,—and call it square!" And before a hand could be raised to prevent him, he had emptied the contents of the carpetbag upon the table.

For a moment his life was in jeopardy. One or two men sprang to their feet, several hands groped for hidden weapons, and a suggestion to "throw him from the window" was only overridden by a gesture from the judge. Tennessee laughed. And apparently oblivious of the excitement, Tennessee's Partner improved the opportunity to mop his face again with his handkerchief.

When order was restored, and the man was made to understand, by the use of forcible figures and rhetoric, that Tennessee's offense could not be condoned by money, his face took a more serious and sanguinary hue, and those who were nearest to him noticed that his rough hand trembled slightly on the table. He hesitated a moment as he slowly returned the gold to the carpetbag, as if he had not yet entirely caught the elevated sense of justice which swayed the tribunal, and was perplexed with the belief that he had not offered enough. Then he turned to the judge, and saying, "This yer is a lone hand, played alone, and without my pardner," he bowed to the jury and was about to withdraw, when the judge called him back:

"If you have anything to say to Tennessee, you had better say it now."

For the first time that evening the eyes of the prisoner and his strange advocate met. Tennessee smiled, showed his white teeth, and saying, "Euchred, old man!" held out his hand. Tennessee's Partner took it in his own, and saying, "I just dropped in as I was passin' to see how things was gettin' on," let the hand passively fall, and adding that "it was a warm night," again mopped his face with his handkerchief, and without another word withdrew.

The two men never again met each other alive. For the unparalleled insult of a bribe offered to Judge Lynch—who, whether bigoted, weak, or narrow, was at least incorruptible—firmly fixed in the mind of that mythical personage any wavering determination of Tennessee's fate; and at the break of day he was marched, closely guarded, to meet it at the top of Marley's Hill.

How he met it, how cool he was, how he refused to say anything, how perfect were the arrangements of the committee, were all duly reported, with the addition of a warning moral and example to all future evil-doers, in the *Red Dog Clarion*, by its editor, who was present, and to whose vigorous English I cheerfully refer the reader. But the beauty of that midsummer morning, the blessed amity of earth and air and sky, the awakened life of the free woods and hills, the joyous renewal and promise of Nature, and above all, the infinite serenity that thrilled through each, was not reported, as not being a part of the social lesson. And yet, when the weak and foolish deed was done, and a life, with its possibilities and responsibilities, had passed out of the misshapen thing that dangled between earth and sky, the birds sang, the flowers bloomed, the sun shone, as cheerily as before; and possibly the *Red Dog Clarion* was right.

Tennessee's Partner was not in the group that surrounded the ominous tree. But as they turned to disperse, attention was drawn to the singular appearance of a motionless donkey cart halted at the side of the road. As they approached, they at once recognized the venerable Jenny and the two-wheeled cart as the property of Tennessee's Partner, used by him in carrying dirt from his claim; and a few paces distant the owner of the equipage himself, sitting under a buckeye tree, wiping the perspiration from his glowing face. In answer to an inquiry, he said he had come for the body of the "diseased," "if it was all the same to the committee." He didn't wish to "hurry anything"; he could "wait." He was not working that day; and when the gentlemen were done with the "diseased," he would take him. "Ef thar is any present," he added, in his simple, serious way, "as would care to jine in the fun'l, they kin come." Perhaps it was from a sense of humor, which I have already intimated was a feature of Sandy Bar—perhaps it was from something even better than that, but two thirds of the loungers accepted the invitation at once.

It was noon when the body of Tennessee was delivered into the hands of his partner. As the cart drew up to the fatal tree, we noticed that it contained a rough oblong box,—apparently made from a section of sluicing,—and half filled with bark and the tassels of pine. The cart was further decorated with slips of willow, and made fragrant with buckeye blossoms. When the body was deposited in the box, Tennessee's Partner drew over it a piece of tarred canvas, and gravely mounting the narrow seat in front, with his feet upon the shafts, urged the little donkey forward. The equipage moved slowly on, at that decorous pace which was habitual with Jenny even under less solemn circumstances. The men—half curiously, half jestingly, but all good-humoredly—strolled along beside the cart, some in advance, some a little in the rear of the homely catafalque. But whether from the narrowing of the road or some present sense of decorum, as the car passed on, the company fell to the rear in couples, keeping step, and otherwise assuming the external show of a formal procession. Jack Folinsbee, who had at the outset played a funeral march in dumb show upon an imaginary trombone, desisted from a lack of sympathy and appreciation—not having, perhaps, your true humorist's capacity to be content with the enjoyment of his own fun.

The way led through Grizzly Cañon, by this time clothed in funereal drapery and shadows. The redwoods, burying their moccasined feet in the red soil, stood in Indian file along the track, trailing an uncouth benediction from their bending boughs upon the passing bier. A hare, surprised into helpless inactivity, sat upright and pulsating in the ferns by the roadside, as the cortège went by. Squirrels hastened to gain a secure outlook from higher boughs; and the bluejays, spreading their wings, fluttered before them like outriders, until the outskirts of Sandy Bar were reached, and the solitary cabin of Tennessee's Partner.

Viewed under more favorable circumstances, it would not have been a cheerful place. The unpicturesque site, the rude and unlovely outlines, the unsavory details, which distinguish the nest-building of the California miner, were all here, with the dreariness of decay superadded. A few paces from the cabin there was a rough enclosure, which, in the brief days of Tennessee's Partner's matrimonial felicity, had been used as a garden, but was now overgrown with fern. As we approached it, we were surprised to find that what we had taken for a recent attempt at cultivation was the broken soil about an open grave.

The cart was halted before the enclosure, and rejecting the offers of assistance with the same air of simple self-reliance he had displayed throughout, Tennessee's Partner lifted the rough coffin on his back, and deposited it unaided within the shallow grave. He then nailed down the board which served as a lid, and mounting the little mound of earth beside it, took off his hat and slowly mopped his face with his handkerchief. This the crowd felt was a preliminary to speech, and they disposed themselves variously on stumps and boulders, and sat expectant.

"When a man," began Tennessee's Partner slowly, "has been running free all day, what's the natural thing for him to do? Why, to come home. And if he ain't in a condition to go home, what can his best friend do? Why, bring him home. And here's Tennessee has been running free, and we brings him home from his wandering." He paused and picked up a fragment of quartz, rubbed it thoughtfully on his sleeve and went on: "It ain't the first time I've packed him on my back, as you see'd me now. It ain't the first time that I brought him to this yer cabin when he couldn't help himself; it ain't the first time that I and Jinny have waited for him on yon hill, and picked him up and so fetched him home, when he couldn't speak and didn't know me. And now that it's the last time, why"—he paused, and rubbed the quartz gently on his sleeve—"you see it's sort of rough on his pardner. And now, gentlemen," he added abruptly, picking up his long-handled shovel, "the fun'l's over; and my thanks, and Tennessee's thanks, to you for your trouble."

Resisting any proffers of assistance, he began to fill in the grave, turning his back upon the crowd, that after a few moments' hesitation gradually withdrew. As they crossed the little ridge that hid Sandy Bar from view, some, looking back, thought they could see Tennessee's Partner, his work done, sitting upon the grave, his shovel between his knees, and his face buried in his red bandana handkerchief. But it was argued by others that you couldn't tell his face from his handkerchief at that distance, and this point remained undecided.

In the reaction that followed the feverish excitement of that day, Tennessee's Partner was not forgotten. A secret investigation had cleared him of any complicity in Tennessee's guilt, and left only a suspicion of his general sanity. Sandy Bar made a point of calling on him, and proffering various uncouth but well-meant kindnesses. But from that day his rude health and great strength seemed visibly to decline; and when the rainy season fairly set in, and the tiny grass blades were beginning to peep from the rocky mound above Tennessee's grave, he took to his bed.

One night, when the pines beside the cabin were swaying in the storm and trailing their slender fingers over the roof, and the roar and rush of the swollen river were heard below, Tennessee's Partner lifted his head from the pillow, saying, "It is time to go for Tennessee; I must put Jinny in the cart"; and would have risen from his bed but for the restraint of his attendant. Struggling, he still pursued his singular fancy: "There, now, steady, Jinny—steady, old girl. How dark it is! Look out for the ruts—and look out for him, too, old gal. Sometimes, you know, when he's blind drunk, he drops down right in the trail. Keep on straight up to the pine on the top of the hill. Thar! I told you so!—thar he is—coming this way, too—all by himself, sober, and his face a-shining. Tennessee! Pardner!"

And so they met.

DEATH OF BILLY THE KID

Charles A. Siringo

In March, 1881, a Deputy United States Marshal by the name of John W. Poe arrived in the booming mining camp of White Oaks. He had been sent to New Mexico by the Cattlemen's Association of the Texas Panhandle. Cattle King Charlie Goodnight, being the president of the association, had selected Mr. Poe as the proper man to put a stop to the stealing of Panhandle cattle by "Billy the Kid" and gang.

After the "Kid's" escape, Pat Garrett went to White Oaks and deputized John W. Poe to assist him in rounding up the "Kid."

From now on Mr. Poe made trips out in the mountains trying to locate the young outlaw. The "Kid's" best friends argued that he was "nobody's fool," and would not remain in the United States, when the Old Mexico border was so near. They didn't realize that little Cupid was shooting his tender young heart full of love-darts, straight from the heart of pretty little Miss Dulcinea del Toboso, of Fort Sumner.

Early in July, Pat Garrett received a letter from an acquaintance by the name of Brazil, in Fort Sumner, advising him that the "Kid" was hanging around there. Garrett at once wrote Brazil to meet him about dark on the night of July 13th at the mouth of the Taiban arroyo, below Fort Sumner.

Now the sheriff took his trusted deputy, John W. Poe, and rode to Roswell, on the Rio Pecos. There they were joined by one of Mr. Garrett's fearless cowboy deputies, "Kip" McKinnie, who had been raised near Uvalde, Texas.

Together the three law officers rode up the river towards Fort Sumner, a distance of eighty miles. They arrived at the mouth of Taiban arroyo an hour after dark on July 13th, but Brazil was not there to meet them. The night was spent sleeping on their saddle blankets.

The next morning Garrett sent Mr. Poe, who was a stranger in the country, and for that reason would not be suspicioned, into Fort Sumner, five miles north, to find out what he could on the sly, about the "Kid's" presence. From Fort Sumner he was to go to Sunny Side, six miles north, to interview a merchant by the name of Mr. Rudolph. Then when the moon was rising, he was to meet Garrett and McKinnie at La Punta de la Glorietta, about four miles north of Fort Sumner.

Failing to find out anything of importance about the "Kid," John W. Poe met his two companions at the appointed place, and they rode into Fort Sumner.

It was about eleven o'clock, and the moon was shining brightly, when the officers rode into an old orchard and concealed their horses. Now the three continued afoot to the home of Pete Maxwell, a wealthy stockman, who was a friend to both Garrett and the "Kid." He lived in a long, one-story adobe building, which had been the U. S. officers' quarters when the soldiers were stationed there. The house fronted south, and had a wide covered porch in front. The grassy front yard was surrounded by a picket fence.

As Pat Garrett had courted his wife and married her in this town, he knew every foot of the ground, even to Pete Maxwell's private bedroom.

On reaching the picket gate, near the corner room, which Pete Maxwell always occupied, Garrett told his two deputies to wait there until after he had a talk with half-breed Pete Maxwell.

The night being hot, Pete Maxwell's door stood wide open, and Garrett walked in.

A short time previous, "Billy the Kid" had arrived from a sheep camp out in the hills. Back of the Maxwell home lived a Mexican servant, who was a warm friend to the "Kid." Here "Billy the Kid" always found late newspapers, placed there by loving hands, for his special benefit.

This old servant had gone to bed. The "Kid" lit a lamp, then pulled off his coat and boots. Now he glanced over the papers to see if his name was mentioned. Finding nothing of interest in the newspapers, he asked the old servant to get up and cook him some supper, as he was very hungry.

Getting up, the servant told him there was no meat in the house. The "Kid" remarked that he would go and get some from Pete Maxwell.

Now he picked up a butcher knife from the table to cut the meat with, and started, bare-footed and bare-headed.

The "Kid" passed within a few feet of the end of the porch where sat John W. Poe and Kip McKinnie. The latter had raised up, when his spur rattled, which attracted the "Kid's" attention. At the same moment Mr. Poe stood up in the small open gateway leading from the street to the end of the porch. They supposed the man coming towards them, only partly dressed, was a servant, or possibly Pete Maxwell.

The "Kid" had pulled his pistol, and so had John Poe, who by that time was almost within arm's reach of the "Kid."

With pistol pointing at Poe, at the same time asking in Spanish: "Quien es?" (Who is that?), he backed into Pete Maxwell's room. He had repeated the above question several times. On entering the room, "Billy the Kid" walked up to within a few feet of Pat Garrett, who was sitting on Maxwell's bed, and asked: "Who are they, Pete?"

Now discovering that a man sat on Pete's bed, the "Kid" with raised pistol pointing towards the bed, began backing across the room.

Pete Maxwell whispered to the sheriff: "That's him, Pat." By this time the "Kid" had backed to a streak of moonlight coming through the south window, asking: "Quien es?" (Who's that?)

Garrett raised his pistol and fired. Then he cocked the pistol again and it went off accidentally, putting a hole in the ceiling, or wall.

Now the sheriff sprang out of the door onto the porch, where stood his two deputies with drawn pistols.

Soon after, Pete Maxwell ran out, and came very near getting a ball from Poe's pistol. Garrett struck the pistol upward, saying: "Don't shoot Maxwell!"

A lighted candle was secured from the mother of Pete Maxwell, who occupied a nearby room, and the dead body of "Billy the Kid" was found stretched out on his back with a bullet wound in his breast, just above the heart. At the right hand lay a Colt's-.41 calibre pistol, and at his left a butcher knife.

Now the native people began to collect—many of them being warm friends of the "Kid's." Garrett allowed them to take the body across the street to a carpenter shop, where it was laid out on a bench. Then lighted candles were placed around the remains of what was once the bravest, and coolest, young outlaw who ever trod the face of the earth.

The next day, this once mother's darling was buried by the side of his chum, Tom O'Fallaher, in the old military cemetery.

He was killed at midnight, July 14th, 1881, being just twenty-one years, seven months and twenty-one days of age, and had killed twenty-one men, not including Indians, which he said didn't count as human beings.

THE BALLAD OF JESSE JAMES

Jesse James was a lad who killed many a man.
He robbed the Glendale train.
He stole from the rich and he gave to the poor,
He'd a hand and a heart and a brain.

Chorus:
> Jesse had a wife to mourn for his life,
> Three children, they were brave,
> But that dirty little coward that shot Mister Howard,
> Has laid Jesse James in his grave.

It was Robert Ford, that dirty little coward,
I wonder how he does feel,
For he ate of Jesse's bread and he slept in Jesse's bed,
Then he laid Jesse James in his grave.

Jesse was a man, a friend to the poor.
He'd never see a man suffer pain,
And with his brother Frank he robbed the Chicago bank,
And stopped the Glendale train.

It was on a Wednesday night, the moon was shining bright,
He stopped the Glendale train,
And the people all did say for many miles away,
It was robbed by Frank and Jesse James.

It was on a Saturday night, Jesse was at home,
Talking to his family brave,
Robert Ford came along like a thief in the night,
And laid Jesse James in his grave.

The people held their breath when they heard of Jesse's death,
And wondered how he ever came to die,

It was one of the gang called little Robert Ford,
That shot Jesse James on the sly.

Jesse went to his rest with hand on his breast,
The devil will be upon his knee,
He was born one day in the county of Shea
And he came of a solitary race.

This song was made by Billy Gashade,
As soon as the news did arrive,
He said there was no man with the law in his hand
Could take Jesse James when alive.

Jesse had a wife to mourn for his life,
Three children, they were brave,
But that dirty little coward that shot Mister Howard,
Has laid Jesse James in his grave.

THE
GREAT CITIES

The metropolises of the United States grew at exhausting speed throughout the nineteenth century. These pieces give a little of the flavor of some of them. Charles Dickens (1812–1870) spent five months touring America in 1842 and wrote his American Notes. *Henry James (1843–1916) wrote* Washington Square *in 1880, but the New York society he describes dates from near the time of Dickens's trip. Theodore Dreiser (1871–1945) described an altogether rougher and more modern urban experience in* Sister Carrie. *When it was published in 1900, it was condemned for immorality, as Caroline Meeber is able to survive in the city unpunished for her misdeeds. Wallace Thurman's novel* Infants of the Spring *describes the artistic community of the Harlem Renaissance, of which he was a part, in New York City after the First World War. Thurman, born in 1902, died in 1934 having written two other novels, including* The Blacker the Berry. *Frank Norris lived an equally brief life (1870–1902). His novel of the murderous dentist,* McTeague (1899), *vividly portrays the San Francisco that existed before the great earthquake and fire of 1906.*

FROM
AMERICAN NOTES
Charles Dickens

BOSTON

To return to Boston. When I got into the streets upon this Sunday morning, the air was so clear, the houses were so bright and gay; the signboards were painted in such gaudy colours; the gilded letters were so very golden; the bricks were so very red, the stone was so very white, the blinds and area railings were so very green, the knobs and plates upon the street doors so marvellously bright and twinkling; and all so slight and unsubstantial in appearance—that every thoroughfare in the city looked exactly like a scene in a pantomime. It rarely happens in the business streets that a tradesman, if I may venture to call anybody a tradesman, where everybody is a merchant, resides above his store; so that many occupations are often carried on in one house, and the whole front is covered with boards and inscriptions. As I walked along, I kept glancing up at these boards, confidently expecting to see a few of them change into something; and I never turned a corner suddenly without looking out for the clown and pantaloon, who, I had no doubt, were hiding in a doorway or behind some pillar close at hand. As to Harlequin and Columbine, I discovered immediately that they lodged (they are always looking after lodgings in a pantomime) at a very small clockmaker's one story high, near the hotel;

which, in addition to various symbols and devices, almost covering the whole front, had a great dial hanging out—to be jumped through, of course.

The suburbs are, if possible, even more unsubstantial-looking than the city. The white wooden houses (so white that it makes one wink to look at them), with their green jalousie blinds, are so sprinkled and dropped about in all directions, without seeming to have any root at all in the ground; and the small churches and chapels are so prim, and bright, and highly varnished; that I almost believed the whole affair could be taken up piecemeal like a child's toy, and crammed into a little box.

The city is a beautiful one, and cannot fail, I should imagine, to impress all strangers very favourably. The private dwelling-houses are, for the most part, large and elegant; the shops extremely good; and the public buildings handsome. The State House is built upon the summit of a hill, which rises gradually at first, and afterwards by a steep ascent, almost from the water's edge. In front is a green enclosure, called the Common. The site is beautiful: and from the top there is a charming panoramic view of the whole town and neighbourhood. In addition to a variety of commodious offices, it contains two handsome chambers; in one the House of Representatives of the State hold their meetings: in the other, the Senate. Such proceedings as I saw here, were conducted with perfect gravity and decorum; and were certainly calculated to inspire attention and respect.

There is no doubt that much of the intellectual refinement and superiority of Boston, is referable to the quiet influence of the University of Cambridge, which is within three or four miles of the city. The resident professors at that university are gentlemen of learning and varied attainments; and are, without one exception that I can call to mind, men who would shed a grace upon, and do honour to, any society in the civilised world. Many of the resident gentry in Boston and its neighbourhood, and I think I am not mistaken in adding, a large majority of those who are attached to the liberal professions there, have been educated at this same school. Whatever the defects of American universities may be, they disseminate no prejudices; rear no bigots; dig up the buried ashes of no old superstitions; never interpose between the people and their improvement; exclude no man because of his religious opinions; above all, in their whole course of study and instruction, recognise a world, and a broad one too, lying beyond the college walls.

It was a source of inexpressible pleasure to me to observe the almost imperceptible, but not less certain effect, wrought by this institution among the small community of Boston; and to note at every turn the humanising tastes and desires it has engendered; the affectionate friendships to which it has given rise; the amount of vanity and prejudice it has dispelled. The golden calf they worship at Boston is a pigmy compared with the giant effigies set up in other parts of that vast countinghouse which lies beyond the Atlantic; and the almighty dollar sinks into something comparatively insignificant, amidst a whole Pantheon of better gods.

Above all, I sincerely believe that the public institutions and charities of this capital of Massachusetts are as nearly perfect, as the most considerate wisdom, benevolence, and humanity, can make them. I never in my life was more affected by the contemplation of happiness, under circumstances of privation and bereavement, than in my visits to these establishments.

* * *

WASHINGTON

We reached Washington at about half-past six that evening, and had upon the way a beautiful view of the Capitol, which is a fine building of the Corinthian order, placed upon a noble and commanding eminence. Arrived at the hotel; I saw no more of the place that night; being very tired, and glad to get to bed.

Breakfast over next morning, I walk about the streets for an hour or two, and, coming home, throw up the window in the front and back, and look out. Here is Washington, fresh in my mind and under my eye.

Take the worst parts of the City Road and Pentonville, or the straggling outskirts of Paris, where the houses are smallest, preserving all their oddities, but especially the small shops and dwellings, occupied in Pentonville (but not in Washington) by furniture-brokers, keepers of poor eating-houses, and fanciers of birds. Burn the whole down; build it up again in wood and plaster; widen it a little; throw in part of

St. John's Wood; put green blinds outside all the private houses, with a red curtain and a white one in every window; plough up all the roads; plant a great deal of coarse turf in every place where it ought *not* to be; erect three handsome buildings in stone and marble, anywhere, but the more entirely out of everybody's way the better; call one the Post Office, one the Patent Office, and one the Treasury; make it scorching hot in the morning, and freezing cold in the afternoon, with an occasional tornado of wind and dust; leave a brick-field without the bricks, in all central places where a street may naturally be expected; and that's Washington.

The hotel in which we live, is a long row of small houses fronting on the street, and opening at the back upon a common yard, in which hangs a great triangle. Whenever a servant is wanted, somebody beats on this triangle from one stroke up to seven, according to the number of the house in which his presence is required; and as all the servants are always being wanted, and none of them ever come, this enlivening engine is in full performance the whole day through. Clothes are drying in the same yard; female slaves, with cotton handkerchiefs twisted round their heads, are running to and fro on the hotel business; black waiters cross and recross with dishes in their hands; two great dogs are playing upon a mound of loose bricks in the centre of the little square; a pig is turning up his stomach to the sun, and grunting "that's comfortable!" and neither the men, nor the women, nor the dogs, nor the pig, nor any created creature, takes the smallest notice of the triangle, which is tingling madly all the time.

I walk to the front window, and look across the road upon a long, straggling row of houses, one story high, terminating, nearly opposite, but a little to the left, in a melancholy piece of waste ground with frowzy grass, which looks like a small piece of country that has taken to drinking, and has quite lost itself. Standing anyhow and all wrong, upon this open space, like something meteoric that has fallen down from the moon, is an odd, lop-sided, one-eyed kind of wooden building, that looks like a church, with a flag-staff as long as itself sticking out of a steeple something larger than a tea-chest. Under the window, is a small stand of coaches, whose slave-drivers are sunning themselves on the steps of our door, and talking idly together. The three most obtrusive houses near at hand, are the three meanest. On one—

a shop, which never has anything in the window, and never has the door open—is painted in large characters, "THE CITY LUNCH." At another, which looks like a backway to somewhere else, but is an independent building in itself, oysters are procurable in every style. At the third, which is a very, very little tailor's shop, pants are fixed to order; or in other words, pantaloons are made to measure. And that is our street in Washington.

It is sometimes called the City of Magnificent Distances, but it might with greater propriety be termed the City of Magnificent Intentions; for it is only on taking a bird's-eye view of it from the top of the Capitol, that one can at all comprehend the vast designs of its projector, an aspiring Frenchman. Spacious avenues, that begin in nothing, and lead nowhere; streets, mile-long, that only want houses, roads and inhabitants; public buildings that need but a public to be complete; and ornaments of great thoroughfares, which only lack great thoroughfares to ornament—are its leading features. One might fancy the season over, and most of the houses gone out of town for ever with their masters. To the admirers of cities it is a Barmecide Feast: a pleasant field for the imagination to rove in; a monument raised to a deceased project, with not even a legible inscription to record its departed greatness.

Such as it is, it is likely to remain. It was originally chosen for the seat of Government, as a means of averting the conflicting jealousies and interests of the different States; and very probably, too, as being remote from mobs; a consideration not to be slighted, even in America. It has no trade or commerce of its own: having little or no population beyond the President and his establishment; the members of the legislature who reside there during the session; the Government clerks and officers employed in the various departments; the keepers of the hotels and boarding-houses; and the tradesmen who supply their tables. It is very unhealthy. Few people would live in Washington, I take it, who were not obliged to reside there; and the tides of emigration and speculation, those rapid and regardless currents, are little likely to flow at any time towards such dull and sluggish water.

The principal features of the Capitol, are, of course, the two houses of Assembly. But there is, besides, in the centre of the building, a fine rotunda, ninety-six feet in diameter, and ninety-six high, whose circular wall is divided into compartments, ornamented by historical pictures. Four of these have for their subjects prominent events in the revolutionary struggle. They were painted by Colonel Trumbull, himself a member of Washington's staff at the time of their occurrence; from which circumstance they derive a peculiar interest of their own. In this same hall Mr. Greenough's large statue of Washington has been lately placed. It has great merits of course, but it struck me as being rather strained and violent for its subject. I could wish, however, to have seen it in a better light than it can ever be viewed in, where it stands.

There is a very pleasant and commodious library in the Capitol; and from a balcony in front, the bird's-eye view, of which I have just spoken, may be had, together with a beautiful prospect of the adjacent country. In one of the ornamented portions of the building, there is a figure of Justice; whereunto the Guide Book says, "the artist at first contemplated giving more of nudity, but he was warned that the public sentiment of this country would not admit of it, and in his caution he has gone, perhaps, into the opposite extreme." Poor Justice! she has been made to wear much stranger garments in America than those she pines in, in the Capitol. Let us hope that she has changed her dressmaker since they were fashioned, and that the public sentiment of the country did not cut out the clothes she hides her lovely figure in, just now.

The House of Representatives is a beautiful and spacious hall, of semicircular shape, supported by handsome pillars. One part of the gallery is appropriated to the ladies, and there they sit in front rows, and come in, and go out, as at a play or concert. The chair is canopied, and raised considerably above the floor of the House; and every member has an easy chair and a writing-desk to himself: which is denounced by some people out of doors as a most unfortunate and injudicious arrangement, tending to long sittings and prosaic speeches. It is an elegant chamber to look at, but a singularly bad one for all purposes of hearing. The Senate, which is smaller, is free from this objection, and is exceedingly well adapted to the uses for which it is designed. The sittings, I need hardly add, take place in the day; and the parliamentary forms are modelled on those of the old country.

FROM

WASHINGTON SQUARE

Henry James

NEW YORK

. . . Doctor Sloper had moved his household gods uptown, as they say in New York. He had been living ever since his marriage in an edifice of red brick, with granite copings and an enormous fanlight over the door, standing in a street within five minutes' walk of the City Hall, which saw its best days (from the social point of view) about 1820. After this, the tide of fashion began to set steadily northward, as, indeed, in New York, thanks to the narrow channel in which it flows, it is obliged to do, and the great hum of traffic rolled farther to the right and left of Broadway. By the time the doctor changed his residence, the murmur of trade had become a mighty uproar, which was music in the ears of all good citizens interested in the commercial development, as they delighted to call it, of their fortunate isle. Doctor Sloper's interest in this phenomenon was only indirect—though, seeing that, as the years went on, half his patients came to be overworked men of business, it might have been more immediate—and when most of his neighbors' dwellings (also ornamented with granite copings and large fanlights) had been converted into offices, warehouses, and shipping agencies, and otherwise applied to the base uses of commerce, he determined to look out for a quieter home. The ideal of quiet and of genteel retirement, in 1835, was found in Washington Square, where the doctor built himself a handsome, modern, wide-fronted house, with a big balcony before the drawing-room windows, and a flight of white marble steps ascending to a portal which was also faced with white marble. This structure, and many of its neighbors, which it exactly resembled, were supposed, forty years ago, to embody the last results of architectural science, and they remain to this day very solid and honorable dwellings. In front of them was the square, containing a considerable quantity of inexpensive vegetation, enclosed by a wooden paling, which increased its rural and accessible appearance; and round the corner was the more august precinct of the Fifth Avenue, taking its origin at this point with a spacious and confident air which already marked it for high destinies. I know not whether it is owing to the tenderness of early associations, but this portion of New York appears to many persons the most delectable. It has a kind of established repose which is not of frequent occurrence in other quarters of the long, shrill city; it has a riper, richer, more honorable look than any of the upper ramifications of the great longitudinal thoroughfare—the look of having had something of a social history. It was here, as you might have been informed on good authority, that you had come into a world which appeared to offer a variety of sources of interest; it was here that your grandmother lived, in venerable solitude, and dispensed a hospitality which commended itself alike to the infant imagination and the infant palate; it was here that you took your first walks abroad, following the nurserymaid with unequal step, and sniffing up the strange odor of the ailanthus trees which at that time formed the principal umbrage of the Square, and diffused an aroma that you were not yet critical enough to dislike as it deserved; it was here, finally, that your first school, kept by a broad-bosomed, broad-based old lady with a ferule, who was always having tea in a blue cup, with a saucer that didn't match, enlarged the circle both of your observations and your sensations. It was here, at any rate, that my heroine spent many years of her life; which is my excuse for this topographical parenthesis.

Mrs. Almond lived much farther uptown, in an embryonic street, with a high number—a region where the extension of the city began to assume a theoretic air, where poplars grew beside the pavement (when there was one), and mingled their shade with the steep roofs of desultory Dutch houses, and where pigs and chickens disported themselves in the gutter. These elements of rural picturesqueness have now wholly departed from New York street scenery; but they were to be found within the memory of middle-aged persons in quarters which now would blush to be reminded of them.

* * *

FROM
SISTER CARRIE
Theodore Dreiser

CHICAGO

Before following her in her round of seeking, let us look at the sphere in which her future was to lie. In 1889 Chicago had the peculiar qualifications of growth which made such adventuresome pilgrimages even on the part of young girls plausible. Its many and growing commercial opportunities gave it widespread fame, which made of it a giant magnet, drawing to itself, from all quarters, the hopeful and the hopeless—those who had their fortune yet to make and those whose fortunes and affairs had reached a disastrous climax elsewhere. It was a city of over 500,000, with the ambition, the daring, the activity of a metropolis of a million. Its streets and houses were already scattered over an area of seventy-five square miles. Its population was not so much thriving upon established commerce as upon the industries which prepared for the arrival of others. The sound of the hammer engaged upon the erection of new structures was everywhere heard. Great industries were moving in. The huge railroad corporations which had long before recognised the prospects of the place had seized upon vast tracts of land for transfer and shipping purposes. Street-car lines had been extended far out into the open country in anticipation of rapid growth. The city had laid miles and miles of streets and sewers through regions where, perhaps, one solitary house stood out alone—a pioneer of the populous ways to be. There were regions open to the sweeping winds and rain, which were yet lighted throughout the night with long, blinking lines of gas-lamps, fluttering in the wind. Narrow board walks extended out, passing here a house, and there a store, at far intervals, eventually ending on the open prairie.

In the central portion was the vast wholesale and shopping district, to which the uninformed seeker for work usually drifted. It was a characteristic of Chicago then, and one not generally shared by other cities, that individual firms of any pretension occupied individual buildings. The presence of ample ground made this possible. It gave an imposing appearance to most of the wholesale houses, whose offices were upon the ground floor and in plain view of the street. The large plates of window glass, now so common, were then rapidly coming into use, and gave to the ground floor offices a distinguished and prosperous look. The casual wanderer could see as he passed a polished array of office fixtures, much frosted glass, clerks hard at work, and genteel business men in "nobby" suits and clean linen lounging about or sitting in groups. Polished brass or nickel signs at the square stone entrances announced the firm and the nature of the business in rather neat and reserved terms. The entire metropolitan centre possessed a high and mighty air calculated to overawe and abash the common applicant, and to make the gulf between poverty and success seem both wide and deep.

Into this important commercial region the timid Carrie went. She walked east along Van Buren Street through a region of lessening importance, until it deteriorated into a mass of shanties and coal-yards, and finally verged upon the river. She walked bravely forward, led by an honest desire to find employment and delayed at every step by the interest of the unfolding scene, and a sense of helplessness amid so much evidence of power and force which she did not understand. These vast buildings, what were they? These strange energies and huge interests, for what purposes were they there? She could have understood the meaning of a little stonecutter's yard at Columbia City, carving little pieces of marble for individual use, but when the yards of some huge stone corporation came into view, filled with spur tracks and flat cars, transpierced by docks from the river and traversed overhead by immense trundling cranes of wood and steel, it lost all significance in her little world.

It was so with the vast railroad yards, with the crowded array of vessels she saw at the river, and the huge factories over the way, lining the water's edge. Through the open windows she could see the figures of men and women in working aprons, moving busily about. The great streets were wall-lined mysteries to her; the vast offices, strange mazes which concerned far-off individuals of importance. She could only think of people connected with them as counting money, dressing magnificently, and riding in carriages. What they dealt in, how they laboured, to what end it all came, she had only the vaguest conception. It was all wonderful, all vast, all far removed, and she sank in spirit inwardly and fluttered feebly at the heart as she thought of entering any one of these mighty concerns and asking for something to do—something that she could do—anything.

NEW YORK

The walk down Broadway, then as now, was one of the remarkable features of the city. There gathered, before the matinée and afterwards, not only all the pretty women who love a showy parade, but the men who love to gaze upon and admire them. It was a very imposing procession of pretty faces and fine clothes. Women appeared in their very best hats, shoes, and gloves, and walked arm in arm on their way to the fine shops or theatres strung along from Fourteenth to Thirty-fourth streets. Equally the men paraded with the very latest they could afford. A tailor might have secured hints on suit measurements, a shoemaker on proper lasts and colours, a hatter on hats. It was literally true that if a lover of fine clothes secured a new suit, it was sure to have its first airing on Broadway. So true and well understood was this fact, that several years later a popular song, detailing this and other facts concerning the afternoon parade on matinée days, and entitled "What Right Has He on Broadway?" was published, and had quite a vogue about the music-halls of the city.

In all her stay in the city, Carrie had never heard of this showy parade; had never been on Broadway when it was taking place. On the other hand, it was a familiar thing to Mrs. Vance, who not only knew of it as an entity, but had often been in it, going purposely to see and be seen, to create a stir with her beauty and dispel any tendency to fall short in dressiness by contrasting herself with the beauty and fashion of the town.

Carrie stepped along easily enough after they got out of the car at Thirty-fourth Street, but soon fixed her eyes upon the lovely company which swarmed by and with them as they proceeded. She noticed suddenly that Mrs. Vance's manner had rather stiffened under the gaze of handsome men and elegantly dressed ladies, whose glances were not modified by any rules of propriety. To stare seemed the proper and natural thing. Carrie found herself stared at and ogled. Men in flawless top-coats, high hats, and silver-headed walking sticks elbowed near and looked too often into conscious eyes. Ladies rustled by in dresses of stiff cloth, shedding affected smiles and perfume. Carrie noticed among them the sprinkling of goodness and the heavy percentage of vice. The rouged and powdered cheeks and lips, the scented hair, the large, misty, and languorous eye, were common enough. With a start she awoke to find that she was in fashion's crowd, on parade in a show place—and such a show place! Jewellers' windows gleamed along the path with remarkable frequency. Florist shops, furriers, haberdashers, confectioners—all followed in rapid succession. The street was full of coaches. Pompous doormen in immense coats, shiny brass belts and buttons, waited in front of expensive salesrooms. Coachmen in tan boots, white tights, and blue jackets waited obsequiously for the mistresses of carriages who were shopping inside. The whole street bore the flavour of riches and show, and Carrie felt that she was not of it. She could not, for the life of her, assume the attitude and smartness of Mrs. Vance, who, in her beauty, was all assurance. She could only imagine that it must be evident to many that she was the less handsomely dressed of the two. It cut her to the quick, and she resolved that she would not come here again until she looked better. At the same time she longed to feel the delight of parading here as an equal. Ah, then she would be happy!

BROOKLYN

On this the fourth day of the strike, the situation had taken a turn for the worse. The strikers, following the counsel of their leaders and the newspapers, had struggled peaceably enough. There had been no great violence done. Cars had been stopped, it is true, and the men argued with. Some crews had been won over and led away, some windows broken, some jeering and yelling done; but in no more than five or six instances had men been seriously injured. These by crowds whose acts the leaders disclaimed.

Idleness, however, and the sight of the company, backed by the police, triumphing, angered the men. They saw that each day more cars were going on, each day more declarations were being made by the company officials that the effective opposition of the strikers was broken. This put desperate thoughts in the minds of the men. Peaceful methods meant, they saw, that the companies would soon run all their cars and those who had complained would be forgotten. There was nothing so helpful to the companies as peaceful methods.

All at once they blazed forth, and for a week there was storm and stress. Cars were assailed, men attacked, policemen struggled with, tracks torn up, and shots fired, until at last street fights and mob movements became frequent, and the city was invested with militia.

Hurstwood knew nothing of the change of temper.

"Run your car out," called the foreman, waving a vigorous hand at him. A green conductor jumped up behind and rang the bell twice as a signal to start. Hurstwood turned the lever and ran the car out through the door into the street in front of the barn. Here two brawny policemen got up beside him on the platform—one on either hand.

At the sound of a gong near the barn door, two bells were given by the conductor and Hurstwood opened his lever.

The two policemen looked about them calmly.

" 'Tis cold, all right, this morning," said the one on the left, who possessed a rich brogue.

"I had enough of it yesterday," said the other. "I wouldn't want a steady job of this."

"Nor I."

Neither paid the slightest attention to Hurstwood, who stood facing the cold wind, which was chilling him completely, and thinking of his orders.

"Keep a steady gait," the foreman had said. "Don't stop for any one who doesn't look like a real passenger. Whatever you do, don't stop for a crowd."

The two officers kept silent for a few moments.

"The last man must have gone through all right," said the officer on the left. "I don't see his car anywhere."

"Who's on there?" asked the second officer, referring, of course, to its complement of policemen.

"Schaeffer and Ryan."

There was another silence, in which the car ran smoothly along. There were not so many houses along this part of the way. Hurstwood did not see many people either. The situation was not wholly disagreeable to him. If he were not so cold, he thought he would do well enough.

He was brought out of this feeling by the sudden appearance of a curve ahead, which he had not expected. He shut off the current and did an energetic turn at the brake, but not in time to avoid an unnaturally quick turn. It shook him up and made him feel like making some apologetic remarks, but he refrained.

"You want to look out for them things," said the officer on the left, condescendingly.

"That's right," agreed Hurstwood, shamefacedly.

"There's lots of them on this line," said the officer on the right.

Around the corner a more populated way appeared. One or two pedestrians were in view ahead. A boy coming out of a gate with a tin milk bucket gave Hurstwood his first objectionable greeting.

"Scab!" he yelled. "Scab!"

Hurstwood heard it, but tried to make no comment, even to himself. He knew he would get that, and much more of the same sort, probably.

At a corner farther up a man stood by the track and signalled the car to stop.

"Never mind him," said one of the officers. "He's up to some game."

Hurstwood obeyed. At the corner he saw the wisdom of it. No sooner did the man perceive the intention to ignore him, than he shook his fist.

"Ah, you bloody coward!" he yelled.

Some half dozen men, standing on the corner, flung taunts and jeers after the speeding car.

Hurstwood winced the least bit. The real thing was slightly worse than the thoughts of it had been.

Now came in sight, three or four blocks farther on, a heap of something on the track.

"They've been at work, here, all right," said one of the policemen.

"We'll have an argument, maybe," said the other.

Hurstwood ran the car close and stopped. He had not done so wholly, however, before a crowd gathered about. It was composed of ex-motormen and conductors in part, with a sprinkling of friends and sympathisers.

"Come off the car, pardner," said one of the men in a voice meant to be conciliatory. "You don't want to take the bread out of another man's mouth, do you?"

Hurstwood held to his brake and lever, pale and very uncertain what to do.

"Stand back," yelled one of the officers, leaning over the platform railing. "Clear out of this, now. Give the man a chance to do his work."

"Listen, pardner," said the leader, ignoring the policeman and addressing Hurstwood. "We're all working men, like yourself. If you were a regular motorman, and had been treated as we've been, you wouldn't want any one to come in and take your place, would you? You wouldn't want any one to do you out of your chance to get your rights, would you?"

"Shut her off! shut her off!" urged the other of the policemen, roughly. "Get out of this, now," and he jumped the railing and landed before the crowd and began shoving. Instantly the other officer was down beside him.

"Stand back, now," they yelled. "Get out of this. What the hell do you mean? Out, now."

It was like a small swarm of bees.

"Don't shove me," said one of the strikers, determinedly. "I'm not doing anything."

"Get out of this!" cried the officer, swinging his club. "I'll give ye a bat on the sconce. Back, now."

"What the hell!" cried another of the strikers, pushing the other way, adding at the same time some lusty oaths.

Crack came an officer's club on his forehead. He blinked his eyes blindly a few times, wabbled on his legs, threw up his hands, and staggered back. In return, a swift fist landed on the officer's neck.

Infuriated by this, the latter plunged left and right, laying about madly with his club. He was ably assisted by his brother of the blue, who poured ponderous oaths upon the troubled waters. No severe damage was done, owing to the agility of the strikers in keeping out of reach. They stood about the sidewalk now and jeered.

"Where is the conductor?" yelled one of the officers, getting his eye on that individual, who had come nervously forward to stand by Hurstwood. The latter had stood gazing upon the scene with more astonishment than fear.

"Why don't you come down here and get these stones off the track?" inquired the officer. "What you standing there for? Do you want to stay here all day? Get down."

Hurstwood breathed heavily in excitement and jumped down with the nervous conductor as if he had been called.

"Hurry up, now," said the other policeman.

Cold as it was, these officers were hot and mad. Hurstwood worked with the conductor, lifting stone after stone and warming himself by the work.

"Ah, you scab, you!" yelled the crowd. "You coward! Steal a man's job, will you? Rob the poor, will you, you thief? We'll get you yet, now. Wait."

Not all of this was delivered by one man. It came from here and there, incorporated with much more of the same sort and curses.

"Work, you blackguards," yelled a voice. "Do the dirty work. You're the suckers that keep the poor people down!"

"May God starve ye yet," yelled an old Irish woman, who now threw open a nearby window and stuck out her head.

"Yes, and you," she added, catching the eye of one of the policemen. "You bloody, murtherin' thafe! Crack my son over the head, will you, you hard-hearted, murtherin' divil? Ah, ye——"

But the officer turned a deaf ear.

"Go to the devil, you old hag," he half muttered as he stared round upon the scattered company.

Now the stones were off, and Hurstwood took his place again amid a continued chorus of epithets. Both officers got up beside him and the conductor rang the bell, when, bang! bang! through window and door came rocks and stones. One narrowly grazed Hurstwood's head. Another shattered the window behind.

"Throw open your lever," yelled one of the officers, grabbing at the handle himself.

Hurstwood complied and the car shot away, followed by a rattle of stones and a rain of curses.

"That —— —— —— hit me in the neck," said one of the officers. "I gave him a good crack for it, though."

"I think I must have left spots on some of them," said the other.

"I know that big guy that called us a —— —— —— ——," said the first. "I'll get him yet for that."

"I thought we were in for it sure, once there," said the second.

Hurstwood, warmed and excited, gazed steadily ahead. It was an astonishing experience for him. He had read of these things, but the reality seemed something altogether new. He was no coward in spirit. The fact that he had suffered this much now rather operated to arouse a stolid determination to stick it out. He did not recur in thought to New York or the flat. This one trip seemed a consuming thing.

They now ran into the business heart of Brooklyn uninterrupted. People gazed at the broken windows of the car and at Hurstwood in his plain clothes. Voices called "scab" now and then, as well as other epithets, but no crowd attacked the car. At the downtown end of the line, one of the officers went to call up his station and report the trouble.

"There's a gang out there," he said, "laying for us yet. Better send some one over there and clean them out."

The car ran back more quietly—hooted, watched, flung at, but not attacked. Hurstwood breathed freely when he saw the barns.

"Well," he observed to himself, "I came out of that all right."

FROM

INFANTS OF THE SPRING

Wallace Thurman

NEW YORK

Stephen had been in New York for a month now, and most of that month had been spent in company with Raymond. Their friendship had become something precious, inviolate and genuine. They had become as intimate in that short period as if they had known one another since childhood. In fact, there was something delightfully naïve and childlike about their frankly acknowledged affection for one another. Like children, they seemed to be totally unconscious of their racial difference. It did not matter that Stephen's ancestors were blond Norsemen, steeped in the tradition of the sagas, and that Raymond's ancestors were a motley ensemble without cultural bonds. It made no difference between them that one was black and the other white. There was something deeper than mere surface color which drew them together, something more vital and lasting than the shallow attraction of racial opposites.

   Their greatest joy came when they could be alone together and talk ... talk about any and everything. They seemed to have so much to say to one another, so much that had remained unsaid all of their respective lives because they had never met anyone else with whom they could converse unreservedly. And no matter how often these conversational communings occurred, no matter how long they lasted, there always seemed to be much more to say.

Stephen was absorbed in learning about Harlem and about Negroes. Raymond was intrigued by the virile Icelandic sagas which Stephen read in the original and translated for his benefit. And both of them were eager to air their thoughts about literature. . . .

Ulysses was a swamp out of which stray orchids grew. Hemingway exemplified the spirit of the twenties in America more vividly than any other contemporary American novelist. To Raymond, Thomas Mann and Andre Gide were the only living literary giants. Andre Gide was not on Stephen's list, but Sigrid Undset was. Neither liked Shaw. They agreed that Dostoievsky was the greatest novelist of all time, but Stephen had only contempt for Marcel Proust whom Raymond swore by, but didn't read. Stendhal, Flaubert and Hardy were discussed amicably, but the sparks flew when they discussed Tolstoi or Zola. And at the mention of Joyce's *Dubliners* and *A Portrait of the Artist as a Young Man* both grew incontinently rhapsodic. "And Hamsun: You mean you haven't read *Hunger,* Ray? God's teeth, man, that's literature."

Their likes and dislikes in literature were sufficiently similar to give them similar philosophies about life, and sufficiently dissimilar to provide food for animated discussions. It was only when their talk veered to Harlem that they found themselves sitting at opposite poles.

Raymond prided himself on knowing all the ins and outs of Harlem. He had been resident there for over three years, during which time he had explored every nook and cranny of that phenomenal Negro settlement. It had, during this period, attained international fame, deservedly, Raymond thought. But he was disgusted with the way everyone sought to romanticize Harlem and Harlem Negroes. And it annoyed him considerably when Stephen began to do likewise. Together they had returned to the spots which Raymond had ferreted out before. They visited all of the cabarets, the speakeasies, the private clubs, the theaters, the back street rendezvous. Stephen was uncritical in his admiration for everything Negroid that he saw. All of the entertainers, musicians, singers, and actors were . . . marvelous. So were all the other Negroes who seemed to be accomplishing one thing or the other. Stephen, like all other whites who had only a book knowledge of Negroes, seemed surprised that a people who had so long been en-slaved, and so recently freed, could make such progress. Raymond tried to explain to Stephen that there was nothing miraculous about the matter.

"Can't you understand, Steve," he would say, "that the Negro had to make what progress he has made or else he wouldn't have survived? He's merely tried to keep the pace set by his environment. People rave about the progress of the Negro. It is nothing near as remarkable, that is generally, as the progress made by foreign immigrants who also come to this country to find freedom from a state of serfdom and illit-eracy just as stringent as that of the pre- and post-Civil War Negro. And as for Harlem. It's bound to be a startling and wondrous commu-nity. Is it not part and parcel of the greatest city in the world? Is it any more remarkable than the Ghetto or Chinatown or the Bronx? It has the same percentage of poverty, middle class endeavor, family life, and underworld, functioning under the same conditions which makes city life a nightmare to any group which is economically insecure. New York is a world within itself, and every new portion of it which gets discovered by the sophisticates and holds the spotlight, seems more unusual than that which has been discovered before."

"Jesus Christ, Ray, you don't appreciate the place. You're too much a part of it."

"Me a part of Harlem? How come?"

"You know what I mean."

"But I don't."

"Well, you live here. You've always lived here."

"Three years isn't always, Steve, even though it may seem like a life-time."

"You're quibbling now."

"I'm not quibbling. The fault lies with you. Just because you've overcome your initial fear of the place and become fascinated by a new and bizarre environment, should you lose your reason? Harlem is New York. Please don't let the fact that it's black New York obscure your vision."

"You're both cynical and silly."

"Granted. But if you had lived in Harlem as long as I have, you would realize that Negroes are much like any other human beings.

They have the same social, physical and intellectual divisions. You're only being intrigued, as I have said before, by the newness of the thing. You should live here a while."

"That's just what I'd like to do."

"Well . . . why not?"

"By jove, that's an idea. I'll move in with you."

"Move in with me?"

"Sure. I much prefer this room to the one I have now, and certainly prefer your company to that of those nincompoops at the International House."

"White people don't live in Harlem."

"Why not?"

"It just isn't done, that's all. What would your friends say?"

"You're the only friend I give a damn about. If you want me, I don't see why I shouldn't live here."

"There isn't any reason why you shouldn't, but . . ."

"But hell, I'm moving in tomorrow. O. K.?"

"I'll be damn glad to have you, Steve."

Twenty-four hours later, Stephen had moved to Harlem.

FROM

McTeague

Frank Norris

SAN FRANCISCO

The street never failed to interest him. It was one of those cross streets peculiar to Western cities, situated in the heart of the residence quarter, but occupied by small tradespeople who lived in the rooms above their shops. There were corner drug stores with huge jars of red, yellow, and green liquids in their windows, very brave and gay; stationers' stores, where illustrated weeklies were tacked upon bulletin boards; barber shops with cigar stands in their vestibules; sad-looking plumbers' offices; cheap restaurants, in whose windows one saw piles of unopened oysters weighted down by cubes of ice, and china pigs and cows knee deep in layers of white beans. At one end of the street McTeague could see the huge power-house of the cable line. Immediately opposite him was a great market; while farther on, over the chimney stacks of the intervening houses, the glass roof of some huge public baths glittered like crystal in the afternoon sun. Underneath him the branch post-office was opening its doors, as was its custom between two and three o'clock on Sunday afternoons. An acrid odor of ink rose upward to him. Occasionally a cable car passed, trundling heavily, with a strident whirring of jostled glass windows.

On week days the street was very lively. It woke to its work about seven o'clock, at the time when the newsboys made their appearance together with the day laborers. The laborers went trudging past in a straggling file—plumbers' apprentices, their pockets stuffed with sections of lead pipe, tweezers, and pliers; carpenters, carrying nothing but their little pasteboard lunch baskets painted to imitate leather; gangs of street workers, their overalls soiled with yellow clay, their picks and long-handled shovels over their shoulders; plasterers, spotted with lime from head to foot. This little army of workers, tramping steadily in one direction, met and mingled with other toilers of a different description—conductors and "swing men" of the cable company going on duty; heavy-eyed night clerks from the drug stores on their way home to sleep; roundsmen returning to the precinct police station to make their night report, and Chinese market gardeners teetering past under their heavy baskets. The cable cars began to fill up; all along the street could be seen the shop keepers taking down their shutters.

Between seven and eight the street breakfasted. Now and then a waiter from one of the cheap restaurants crossed from one sidewalk to the other, balancing on one palm a tray covered with a napkin. Everywhere was the smell of coffee and of frying steaks. A little later, following in the path of the day laborers, came the clerks and shop girls, dressed with a certain cheap smartness, always in a hurry, glancing apprehensively at the power-house clock. Their employers followed an hour or so later—on the cable cars for the most part—whiskered gentlemen with huge stomachs, reading the morning papers with great gravity; bank cashiers and insurance clerks with flowers in their buttonholes.

At the same time the school children invaded the street, filling the air with a clamor of shrill voices, stopping at the stationers' shops, or idling a moment in the doorways of the candy stores. For over half an hour they held possession of the sidewalks, then suddenly disappeared, leaving behind one or two stragglers who hurried along with great strides of their little thin legs, very anxious and preoccupied.

Towards eleven o'clock the ladies from the great avenue a block above Polk Street made their appearance, promenading the sidewalks leisurely, deliberately. They were at their morning's marketing. They were handsome women, beautifully dressed. They knew by name their butchers and grocers and vegetable men. From his window McTeague saw them in front of the stalls, gloved and veiled and daintily shod, the subservient provision-men at their elbows, scribbling hastily in the order books. They all seemed to know one another, these grand ladies from the fashionable avenue. Meetings took place here and there; a conversation was begun; others arrived; groups were formed; little impromptu receptions were held before the chopping blocks of butchers' stalls, or on the sidewalk, around boxes of berries and fruit.

From noon to evening the population of the street was of a mixed character. The street was busiest at that time; a vast and prolonged murmur arose—the mingled shuffling of feet, the rattle of wheels, the heavy trundling of cable cars. At four o'clock the school children once more swarmed the sidewalks, again disappearing with surprising suddenness. At six the great homeward march commenced; the cars were crowded, the laborers thronged the sidewalks, the newsboys chanted the evening papers. Then all at once the street fell quiet; hardly a soul was in sight; the sidewalks were deserted. It was supper hour. Evening began; and one by one a multitude of lights, from the demoniac glare of the druggists' windows to the dazzling blue whiteness of the electric globes, grew thick from street corner to street corner. Once more the street was crowded. Now there was no thought but for amusement. The cable cars were loaded with theatre-goers—men in high hats and young girls in furred opera cloaks. On the sidewalks were groups and couples—the plumbers' apprentices, the girls of the ribbon counters, the little families that lived on the second stories over their shops, the dressmakers, the small doctors, the harness makers—all the various inhabitants of the street were abroad, strolling idly from shop window to shop window, taking the air after the day's work. Groups of girls collected on the corners, talking and laughing very loud, making remarks upon the young men that passed them. The *tamale* men appeared. A band of Salvationists began to sing before a saloon.

Then, little by little, Polk Street dropped back to solitude. Eleven o'clock struck from the powerhouse clock. Lights were extinguished. At one o'clock the cable stopped, leaving an abrupt silence in the air. All at once it seemed very still. The only noises were the occasional footfalls of a policeman and the persistent calling of ducks and geese in the closed market. The street was asleep.

AMERICANS

It stands to reason that a staple of the material poets and writers use in their work is to be found in the people they see around them. "I Hear America Singing" was one of the many poems Walt Whitman (1819–1892) added to Leaves of Grass *after it was first published. The work contained twelve poems in its first edition of 1855 and 383 in the final "Deathbed Edition" of 1892. There are innumerable version of the Casey Jones song, but all tell of the heroism of John Luther "Casey" Jones. Herman Melville (1819–1891) published his masterpiece* Moby Dick *in 1851. Melville had worked on ships in the South Seas and drew from his experiences. In 1883 Willa Cather (1873–1947) moved with her family from Virginia to the Nebraska town of Red Cloud. When she later came to write fiction, she remembered the frontier people she had encountered, most notably in the novels* O Pioneers! *(1913) and* My Ántonia *(1918) and stories like "The Enchanted Bluff." The radical writer and politician Upton Sinclair (1878–1968) earned his literary breakthrough with* The Jungle *when it was published in 1906. It is one of the few novels to have changed the world it depicts: The appalling conditions the immigrant workers faced in the Chicago meat-packing industry, as highlighted in his book, helped lead to the passage of pure-food laws.*

I HEAR AMERICA SINGING

Walt Whitman

I hear America singing, the varied carols I hear,
Those of mechanics, each one singing his as it should be
    blithe and strong,
The carpenter singing his as he measures his plank or
    beam,
The mason singing his as he makes ready for work, or
    leaves off work,
The boatman singing what belongs to him in his boat, the
    deckhand singing on the steamboat deck,
The shoemaker singing as he sits on his bench, the hatter
    singing as he stands,
The wood-cutter's song, the ploughboy's on his way in
    the morning, or at noon intermission or at sundown,
The delicious singing of the mother, or of the young wife
    at work, or of the girl sewing or washing,
Each singing what belongs to him or her and to none else,
The day what belongs to the day—at night the party of
    young fellows, robust, friendly,
Singing with open mouths their strong melodious songs.

CASEY JONES

(Trad.)

Come all you rounders for I want you to hear
The story told of a brave engineer;
Casey Jones was the rounder's name
On a heavy six-eight wheeler he rode to fame.

Caller called Jones about half-past four,
Jones kissed his wife at the station door,
Climbed into the cab with the orders in his hand,
Says, "This is my trip to the promised land."

Through South Memphis yards on the fly,
He heard the fireman say, "You've got a white-eye,"

All the switchmen knew by the engine's moans,
That the man at the throttle was Casey Jones.

It had been raining for more than a week,
The railroad track was like the bed of a creek.
They rated him down to a thirty mile gait,
Threw the south-bound mail about eight hours late.

Fireman says, "Casey, you're runnin' too fast,
You run the block signal the last station you passed."
Jones says, "Yes, I think we can make it though,
For she steams much better than ever I know."

Jones says, "Fireman, don't you fret,
Keep knockin' at the firedoor, don't give up yet;
I'm goin' to run her till she leaves the rail
Or make it on time with the south-bound mail."

Around the curve and a-down the dump
Two locomotives were a-bound to bump.

Fireman hollered, "Jones, it's just ahead,
We might jump and make it but we'll all be dead."

'Twas around this curve he saw a passenger train;
Something happened in Casey's brain;
Fireman jumped off, but Casey stayed on,
He's a good engineer but he's dead and gone—

Poor Casey was always all right,
He stuck to his post both day and night;
They loved to hear the whistle of old Number Three
As he came into Memphis on the old K.C.

Headaches and heartaches and all kinds of pain
Are not apart from a railroad train;
Tales that are earnest, noble and gran'
Belong to the life of a railroad man.

MOBY DICK

Herman Melville

THE STREET

If I had been astonished at first catching a glimpse of so outlandish an individual as Queequeg circulating among the polite society of a civilized town, that astonishment soon departed upon taking my first daylight stroll through the streets of New Bedford.

In thoroughfares nigh the docks, any considerable seaport will frequently offer to view the queerest looking nondescripts from foreign parts. Even in Broadway and Chestnut streets, Mediterranean mariners will sometimes jostle the affrighted ladies. Regent street is not unknown to Lascars and Malays; and at Bombay, in the Apollo Green, live Yankees have often scared the natives. But New Bedford beats all Water street and Wapping. In these last-mentioned haunts you see only sailors; but in New Bedford, actual cannibals stand chatting at street corners; savages outright; many of whom yet carry on their bones unholy flesh. It makes a stranger stare.

But, besides the Feegeeans, Tongatabooarrs, Erromanggoans, Pannangians, and Brighggians, and, besides the wild specimens of the whaling-craft which unheeded reel about the streets, you will see other sights still more curious, certainly more comical. There weekly arrive in this town scores of green Vermonters and New Hampshire men, all athirst for gain and glory in the fishery. They are mostly young, of stalwart frames; fellows who have felled forests, and now seek to drop the axe and snatch the whale-lance. Many are as green as the Green Mountains whence they came. In some things you would think them but a few hours old. Look there! that chap strutting round the corner. He wears a beaver hat and swallow-tailed coat, girdled with a sailor-belt and sheath-knife. Here comes another with a sou'-wester and a bombazine cloak.

No town-bred dandy will compare with a country-bred one—I mean a downright bumpkin dandy—a fellow that, in the dog-days, will mow his two acres in buckskin gloves for fear of tanning his hands. Now when a country dandy like this takes it into his head to make a distinguished reputation, and joins the great whale-fishery, you should see the comical things he does upon reaching the seaport. In bespeaking his sea-outfit, he orders bell-buttons to his waistcoats; straps to his canvas trowsers. Ah, poor Hay-Seed! how bitterly will burst those straps in the first howling gale, when thou art driven, straps, buttons, and all, down the throat of the tempest.

But think not that this famous town has only harpooneers, cannibals, and bumpkins to show her visitors. Not at all. Still New Bedford is a queer place. Had it not been for us whalemen, that tract of land would this day perhaps have been in as howling condition as the coast of Labrador. As it is, parts of her back country are enough to frighten one, they look so bony. The town itself is perhaps the dearest place to live in, in all New England. It is a land of oil, true enough: but not like Canaan; a land, also, of corn and wine. The streets do not run with milk; nor in the spring-time do they pave them with fresh eggs. Yet, in spite of this, nowhere in all America will you find more patrician-like houses; parks and gardens more opulent, than in New Bedford. Whence came they? how planted upon this once scraggy scoria of a country?

Go and gaze upon the iron emblematical harpoons round yonder lofty mansion, and your question will be answered. Yes; all these brave houses and flowery gardens came from the Atlantic, Pacific, and Indian oceans. One and all, they were harpooned and dragged up hither from the bottom of the sea. Can Herr Alexander perform a feat like that?

In New Bedford, fathers, they say, give whales for dowers to their daughters, and portion off their nieces with a few porpoises a-piece. You must go to New Bedford to see a brilliant wedding; for, they say, they have reservoirs of oil in every house, and every night recklessly burn their lengths in spermaceti candles.

In summer time, the town is sweet to see; full of fine maples—long avenues of green and gold. And in August, high in air, the beautiful and bountiful horse-chestnuts, candelabra-wise, proffer the passer-by their tapering upright cones of congregated blossoms. So omnipotent is art; which in many a district of New Bedford has superinduced bright terraces of flowers upon the barren refuse rocks thrown aside at creation's final day.

And the women of New Bedford, they bloom like their own red roses. But roses only bloom in summer; whereas the fine carnation of their cheeks is perennial as sunlight in the seventh heavens. Elsewhere match that bloom of theirs, ye cannot, save in Salem, where they tell me the young girls breathe such musk, their sailor sweethearts smell them miles off shore, as though they were drawing nigh the odorous Moluccas instead of the Puritanic sands.

The Enchanted Bluff

Willa Cather

We had our swim before sundown, and while we were cooking our supper the oblique rays of light made a dazzling glare on the white sand about us. The translucent red ball itself sank behind the brown stretches of cornfield as we sat down to eat, and the warm layer of air that had rested over the water and our clean sand bar grew fresher and smelled of the rank ironweed and sunflowers growing on the flatter shore. The river was brown and sluggish, like any other of the half-dozen streams that water the Nebraska corn lands. On one shore was an irregular line of bald clay bluffs where a few scrub oaks with thick trunks and flat, twisted tops threw light shadows on the long grass. The western shore was low and level, with cornfields that stretched to the skyline, and all along the water's edge were little sandy coves and beaches where slim cottonwoods and willow saplings flickered.

The turbulence of the river in springtime discouraged milling, and, beyond keeping the old red bridge in repair, the busy farmers did not concern themselves with the stream; so the Sandtown boys were left in undisputed possession. In the autumn we hunted quail through the miles of stubble and fodder land along the flat shore, and, after the winter skating season was over and the ice had gone out, the spring freshets and flooded bottoms gave us our great excitement of the year. The channel was never the same for two successive seasons. Every spring the swollen stream undermined a bluff to the east, or bit out a few acres of cornfield to the west and whirled the soil away to deposit it in spumy mud banks somewhere else. When the water fell low in midsummer, new sand bars were thus exposed to dry and whiten in the August sun. Sometimes these were banked so firmly that the fury of the next freshet failed to unseat them; the little willow seedlings emerged triumphantly from the yellow froth, broke into spring leaf, shot up into summer growth, and with their mesh of roots bound together the moist sand beneath them against the batterings of another April. Here and there a cottonwood soon glittered among them, quivering in the low current of air that, even on breathless days when the dust hung like smoke above the wagon road, trembled along the face of the water.

It was on such an island, in the third summer of its yellow green, that we built our watch fire; not in the thicket of dancing willow wands, but on the level terrace of fine sand which had been added that spring; a little new bit of world, beautifully ridged with ripple marks, and strewn with the tiny skeletons of turtles and fish, all as white and dry as if they had been expertly cured. We had been careful not to mar the freshness of the place, although we often swam to it on summer evenings and lay on the sand to rest.

This was our last watch fire of the year, and there were reasons why I should remember it better than any of the others. Next week the other boys were to file back to their old places in the Sandtown High School, but I was to go up to the Divide to teach my first country school in the Norwegian district. I was already homesick at the thought of quitting the boys with whom I had always played; of leaving the river, and going up into a windy plain that was all windmills and cornfields and big pastures; where there was nothing wilful or unmanageable in the landscape, no new islands, and no chance of unfamiliar birds—such as often followed the watercourses.

Other boys came and went and used the river for fishing or skating, but we six were sworn to the spirit of the stream, and we were friends mainly because of the river. There were the two Hassler boys, Fritz and Otto, sons of the little German tailor. They were the youngest of us; ragged boys of ten and twelve, with sunburned hair, weather-stained faces, and pale blue eyes. Otto, the elder, was the best mathe-

matician in school, and clever at his books, but he always dropped out
in the spring term as if the river could not get on without him. He and
Fritz caught the fat, horned catfish and sold them about the town, and
they lived so much in the water that they were as brown and sandy as
the river itself.

There was Percy Pound, a fat, freckled boy with chubby cheeks,
who took half a dozen boys' story-papers and was always being kept in
for reading detective stories behind his desk. There was Tip Smith,
destined by his freckles and red hair to be the buffoon in all our games,
though he walked like a timid little old man and had a funny, cracked
laugh. Tip worked hard in his father's grocery store every afternoon,
and swept it out before school in the morning. Even his recreations
were laborious. He collected cigarette cards and tin tobacco-tags in-
defatigably, and would sit for hours humped up over a snarling little
scroll-saw which he kept in his attic. His dearest possessions were
some little pill bottles that purported to contain grains of wheat from
the Holy Land, water from the Jordan and the Dead Sea, and earth
from the Mount of Olives. His father had bought these dull things
from a Baptist missionary who peddled them, and Tip seemed to derive great satisfaction from their remote origin.

The tall boy was Arthur Adams. He had fine hazel eyes that were almost too reflective and sympathetic for a boy, and such a pleasant
voice that we all loved to hear him read aloud. Even when he had to
read poetry aloud at school, no one ever thought of laughing. To be
sure, he was not at school very much of the time. He was seventeen
and should have finished the High School the year before, but he was
always off somewhere with his gun. Arthur's mother was dead, and his
father, who was feverishly absorbed in promoting schemes, wanted to
send the boy away to school and get him off his hands; but Arthur always begged off for another year and promised to study. I remember
him as a tall, brown boy with an intelligent face, always lounging
among a lot of us little fellows, laughing at us oftener than with us, but
such a soft, satisfied laugh that we felt rather flattered when we provoked it. In after-years people said that Arthur had been given to evil
ways as a lad, and it is true that we often saw him with the gambler's
sons and with old Spanish Fanny's boy, but if he learned anything ugly
in their company he never betrayed it to us. We would have followed

Arthur anywhere, and I am bound to say that he led us into no worse places than the cattail marshes and the stubble fields. These, then, were the boys who camped with me that summer night upon the sand bar.

After we finished our supper we beat the willow thicket for driftwood. By the time we had collected enough, night had fallen, and the pungent, weedy smell from the shore increased with the coolness. We threw ourselves down about the fire and made another futile effort to show Percy Pound the Little Dipper. We had tried it often before, but he could never be got past the big one.

"You see those three big stars just below the handle, with the bright one in the middle?" said Otto Hassler; "that's Orion's belt, and the bright one is the clasp." I crawled behind Otto's shoulder and sighted up his arm to the star that seemed perched upon the tip of his steady forefinger. The Hassler boys did seine-fishing at night, and they knew a good many stars.

Percy gave up the Little Dipper and lay back on the sand, his hands clasped under his head. "I can see the North Star," he announced, contentedly, pointing toward it with his big toe. "Anyone might get lost and need to know that."

We all looked up at it.

"How do you suppose Columbus felt when his compass didn't point north any more?" Tip asked.

Otto shook his head. "My father says that there was another North Star once, and that maybe this one won't last always. I wonder what would happen to us down here if anything went wrong with it?"

Arthur chuckled. "I wouldn't worry, Ott. Nothing's apt to happen to it in your time. Look at the Milky Way! There must be lots of good dead Indians."

We lay back and looked, meditating, at the dark cover of the world. The gurgle of the water had become heavier. We had often noticed a mutinous, complaining note in it at night, quite different from its cheerful daytime chuckle, and seeming like the voice of a much deeper and more powerful stream. Our water had always these two moods: the one of sunny complaisance, the other of inconsolable, passionate regret.

"Queer how the stars are all in sort of diagrams," remarked Otto.

"You could do most any proposition in geometry with 'em. They always look as if they meant something. Some folks say everybody's fortune is all written out in the stars, don't they?"

"They believe so in the old country," Fritz affirmed.

But Arthur only laughed at him. "You're thinking of Napoleon, Fritzey. He had a star that went out when he began to lose battles. I guess the stars don't keep any close tally on Sandtown folks."

We were speculating on how many times we could count a hundred before the evening star went down behind the cornfields, when someone cried, "There comes the moon, and it's as big as a cart wheel!"

We all jumped up to greet it as it swam over the bluffs behind us. It came up like a galleon in full sail; an enormous, barbaric thing, red as an angry heathen god.

"When the moon came up red like that, the Aztecs used to sacrifice their prisoners on the temple top," Percy announced.

"Go on, Perce. You got that out of *Golden Days*. Do you believe that, Arthur?" I appealed.

Arthur answered, quite seriously: "Like as not. The moon was one of their gods. When my father was in Mexico City he saw the stone where they used to sacrifice their prisoners."

As we dropped down by the fire again some one asked whether the Mound-Builders were older than the Aztecs. When we once got upon the Mound-Builders we never willingly got away from them, and we were still conjecturing when we heard a loud splash in the water.

"Must have been a big cat jumping," said Fritz. "They do sometimes. They must see bugs in the dark. Look what a track the moon makes!"

There was a long, silvery streak on the water, and where the current fretted over a big log it boiled up like gold pieces.

"Suppose there ever *was* any gold hid away in this old river?" Fritz asked. He lay like a little brown Indian, close to the fire, his chin on his hand and his bare feet in the air. His brother laughed at him, but Arthur took his suggestion seriously.

"Some of the Spaniards thought there was gold up here somewhere. Seven cities chuck full of gold, they had it, and Coronado and his men came up to hunt it. The Spaniards were all over this country once."

Percy looked interested. "Was that before the Mormons went through?"

We all laughed at this.

"Long enough before. Before the Pilgrim Fathers, Perce. Maybe they came along this very river. They always followed the water-courses."

"I wonder where this river really does begin?" Tip mused. That was an old and a favorite mystery which the map did not clearly explain. On the map the little black line stopped somewhere in western Kansas; but since rivers generally rose in mountains, it was only reasonable to suppose that ours came from the Rockies. Its destination, we knew, was the Missouri, and the Hassler boys always maintained that we could embark at Sandtown in floodtime, follow our noses, and eventually arrive at New Orleans. Now they took up their old argument. "If us boys had grit enough to try it, it wouldn't take no time to get to Kansas City and St. Joe."

We began to talk about the places we wanted to go to. The Hassler boys wanted to see the stockyards in Kansas City, and Percy wanted to see a big store in Chicago. Arthur was interlocutor and did not betray himself.

"Now it's your turn, Tip."

Tip rolled over on his elbow and poked the fire, and his eyes looked shyly out of his queer, tight little face. "My place is awful far away. My Uncle Bill told me about it."

Tip's Uncle Bill was a wanderer, bitten with mining fever, who had drifted into Sandtown with a broken arm, and when it was well had drifted out again.

"Where is it?"

"Aw, it's down in New Mexico somewheres. There aren't no railroads or anything. You have to go on mules, and you run out of water before you get there and have to drink canned tomatoes."

"Well, go on, kid. What's it like when you do get there?"

Tip sat up and excitedly began his story.

"There's a big red rock there that goes right up out of the sand for about nine hundred feet. The country's flat all around it, and this here rock goes up all by itself, like a monument. They call it the Enchanted Bluff down there, because no white man has ever been on top of it. The sides are smooth rock, and straight up, like a wall. The Indians say that hundreds of years ago, before the Spaniards came, there was a village away up there in the air. The tribe that lived there had some sort of steps, made out of wood and bark, hung down over the face of the bluff, and the braves went down to hunt and carried water up in big jars swung on their backs. They kept a big supply of water and dried meat up there, and never went down except to hunt. They were a peaceful tribe that made cloth and pottery, and they went up there to get out of the wars. You see, they could pick off any war party that tried to get up their little steps. The Indians say they were a handsome people, and they had some sort of queer religion. Uncle Bill thinks they were Cliff-Dwellers who had got into trouble and left home. They weren't fighters, anyhow.

"One time the braves were down hunting and an awful storm came up—a kind of waterspout—and when they got back to their rock they found their little staircase had been all broken to pieces, and only a few steps were left hanging away up in the air. While they were camped at the foot of the rock, wondering what to do, a war party from the north came along and massacred 'em to a man, with all the old folks and women looking on from the rock. Then the war party went on south and left the village to get down the best way they could. Of course they never got down. They starved to death up there, and when the war party came back on their way north, they could hear the children crying from the edge of the bluff where they had crawled out, but they didn't see a sign of a grown Indian, and nobody has ever been up there since."

We exclaimed at this dolorous legend and sat up.

"There couldn't have been many people up there," Percy demurred. "How big is the top, Tip?"

"Oh, pretty big. Big enough so that the rock doesn't look nearly as tall as it is. The top's bigger than the base. The bluff is sort of worn away for several hundred feet up. That's one reason it's so hard to climb."

I asked how the Indians got up, in the first place.

"Nobody knows how they got up or when. A hunting party came along once and saw that there was a town up there, and that was all."

Otto rubbed his chin and looked thoughtful. "Of course there must be some way to get up there. Couldn't people get a rope over someway and pull a ladder up?"

Tip's little eyes were shining with excitement. "I know a way. Me and Uncle Bill talked it over. There's a kind of rocket that would take a rope over—lifesavers use 'em—and then you could hoist a rope ladder and peg it down at the bottom and make it tight with guy ropes on the other side. I'm going to climb that there bluff, and I've got it all planned out."

Fritz asked what he expected to find when he got up there.

"Bones, maybe, or the ruins of their town, or pottery, or some of their idols. There might be 'most anything up there. Anyhow, I want to see."

"Sure nobody else has been up there, Tip?" Arthur asked.

"Dead sure. Hardly anybody ever goes down there. Some hunters tried to cut steps in the rock once, but they didn't get higher than a man can reach. The Bluff's all red granite, and Uncle Bill thinks it's a boulder the glaciers left. It's a queer place, anyhow. Nothing but cactus and desert for hundreds of miles, and yet right under the Bluff there's good water and plenty of grass. That's why the bison used to go down there."

Suddenly we heard a scream above our fire, and jumped up to see a dark, slim bird floating southward far above us—a whooping crane, we knew by her cry and her long neck. We ran to the edge of the island, hoping we might see her alight, but she wavered southward along the rivercourse until we lost her. The Hassler boys declared that by the look of the heavens it must be after midnight, so we threw more wood on our fire, put on our jackets, and curled down in the warm sand. Several of us pretended to doze, but I fancy we were really thinking about Tip's Bluff and the extinct people. Over in the wood the ring doves were calling mournfully to one another, and once we heard a dog bark, far away. "Somebody getting into old Tommy's melon patch," Fritz murmured sleepily, but nobody answered him. By and by Percy spoke out of the shadows.

"Say, Tip, when you go down there will you take me with you?"

"Maybe."

"Suppose one of us beats you down there, Tip?"

"Whoever gets to the Bluff first has got to promise to tell the rest of us exactly what he finds," remarked one of the Hassler boys, and to this we all readily assented.

Somewhat reassured, I dropped off to sleep. I must have dreamed about a race for the Bluff, for I awoke in a kind of fear that other people were getting ahead of me and that I was losing my chance. I sat up in my damp clothes and looked at the other boys, who lay tumbled in uneasy attitudes about the dead fire. It was still dark, but the sky was blue with the last wonderful azure of night. The stars glistened like crystal globes, and trembled as if they shone through a depth of clear water. Even as I watched, they began to pale and the sky brightened. Day came suddenly, almost instantaneously. I turned for another look at the blue night, and it was gone. Everywhere the birds began to call, and all manner of little insects began to chirp and hop about in the willows. A breeze sprang up from the west and brought the heavy smell of ripened corn. The boys rolled over and shook themselves. We stripped and plunged into the river just as the sun came up over the windy bluffs.

When I came home to Sandtown at Christmas time, we skated out to our island and talked over the whole project of the Enchanted Bluff, renewing our resolution to find it.

* * *

Although that was twenty years ago, none of us have ever climbed the Enchanted Bluff. Percy Pound is a stockbroker in Kansas City and will go nowhere that his red touring car cannot carry him. Otto Hassler went on the railroad and lost his foot braking; after which he and Fritz succeeded their father as the town tailors.

Arthur sat about the sleepy little town all his life—he died before he was twenty-five. The last time I saw him, when I was home on one of my college vacations, he was sitting in a steamer chair under a cottonwood tree in the little yard behind one of the two Sandtown saloons. He was very untidy and his hand was not steady, but when he rose, unabashed, to greet me, his eyes were as clear and warm as ever. When I had talked with him for an hour and heard him laugh again, I wondered how it was that when Nature had taken such pains with a man, from his hands to the arch of his long foot, she had ever lost him in Sandtown. He joked about Tip Smith's Bluff, and declared he was going down there just as soon as the weather got cooler; he thought the Grand Canyon might be worth while, too.

I was perfectly sure when I left him that he would never get beyond the high plank fence and the comfortable shade of the cottonwood. And, indeed, it was under that very tree that he died one summer morning.

Tip Smith still talks about going to New Mexico. He married a slatternly, unthrifty country girl, has been much tied to a perambulator, and has grown stooped and grey from irregular meals and broken sleep. But the worst of his difficulties are now over, and he has, as he says, come into easy water. When I was last in Sandtown I walked home with him late one moonlight night, after he had balanced his cash and shut up his store. We took the long way around and sat down on the schoolhouse steps, and between us we quite revived the romance of the lone red rock and the extinct people. Tip insists that he still means to go down there, but he thinks now he will wait until his boy Bert is old enough to go with him. Bert has been let into the story, and thinks of nothing but the Enchanted Bluff.

FROM

THE JUNGLE

Upton Sinclair

With one member trimming beef in a cannery, and another working in a sausage factory, the family had a first-hand knowledge of the great majority of Packingtown swindles. For it was the custom, as they found, whenever meat was so spoiled that it could not be used for anything else, either to can it or else to chop it up into sausages. With what had been told them by Jonas, who had worked in the pickle rooms, they could now study the whole of the spoiled-meat industry on the inside, and read a new and grim meaning into that old Packingtown jest—that they use everything of the pig except the squeal.

Jonas had told them how the meat that was taken out of pickle would often be found sour, and how they would rub it up with soda to take away the smell, and sell it to be eaten on free-lunch counters; also of all the miracles of chemistry which they performed, giving to any sort of meat, fresh or salted, whole or chopped, any colour and any flavour, and any odour they chose. In the pickling of hams they had an ingenious apparatus by which they saved time and increased the capacity of the plant—a machine consisting of a hollow needle attached to a pump; by plunging this needle into the meat and working with his foot, a man could fill a ham with pickle in a few seconds. And yet, in spite of this, there would be hams found spoiled, some of them with an odour so bad that a man could hardly bear to be in the room with them. To pump into these the packers had a second and much stronger pickle which destroyed the odour—a process known to the workers as 'giving them thirty per cent'. Also, after the hams had been smoked, there would be found some that had gone to the bad. Formerly these had been sold as 'Number Three Grade', but later on some ingenious person had hit upon a new device, and now they would extract the bone, about which the bad part generally lay, and insert in the hole a white-hot iron. After this invention there was no longer Number One, Two, and Three Grade—there was only Number One Grade. The packers were always originating such schemes—they had what they called 'boneless hams', which were all the odds and ends of pork stuffed into casings; and 'California hams', which were the shoulders, with big knuckle-joints, and nearly all the meat cut out; and fancy 'skinned hams', which were made of the oldest hogs, whose skins were so heavy and coarse that no one would buy them—that is, until they had been cooked and chopped fine and labelled 'head cheese'!

It was only when the whole ham was spoiled that it came into the department of Elzbieta. Cut up by the two-thousand-revolutions-a-minute flyers, and mixed with half a ton of other meat, no odour that ever was in a ham could make any difference. There was never the least attention paid to what was cut up for sausages; there would come all the way back from Europe old sausage that had been rejected, and that was mouldy and white—it would be dosed with borax and glycerine, and dumped into the hoppers, and made over again for home consumption. There would be meat that had tumbled out on the floor, in the dirt and sawdust, where the workers had trampled and spit uncounted billions of consumption germs. There would be meat stored in great piles in rooms; and the water from leaky roofs would drip over it, and thousands of rats would race about on it. It was too dark in these storage places to see well, but a man could run his hand over these piles of meat and sweep off handfuls of the dried dung of rats. These rats were nuisances, and the packers would put poisoned bread out for them; they would die, and then rats, bread, and meat would go into the hoppers together. This is no fairy story and no joke; the meat would be shovelled into carts, and the man who did the shovelling would not ʳouble to lift out a rat even when he saw one—there were things that ⁿt into the sausage in comparison with which a poisoned rat was a tidbit. There was no place for the men to wash their hands before they ate their dinner, and so they made a practice of washing them in the water that was to be ladled into the sausage. There were the butt ends of smoked meat, and the scraps of corned beef, and all the odds and ends of the waste of the plants, that would be dumped into old barrels in the cellar and left there. Under the system of rigid economy which the packers enforced, there were some jobs that it only paid to do once in a long time, and among these was the cleaning out of the waste barrels. Every spring they did it; and in the barrels would be dirt and rust, and old nails and stale water—and cartload after cartload of it would be taken up and dumped into the hoppers with fresh meat, and sent out to the public's breakfast. Some of it they would make into 'smoked' sausage—but as the smoking took time, and was therefore expensive, they would call upon their chemistry department, and preserve it with borax and colour it with gelatine to make it brown. All of their sausage came out of the same bowl, but when they came to wrap it they would stamp some of it 'special', and for this they would charge two cents more a pound.

* * *

Such were the new surroundings in which Elzbieta was placed, and such was the work she was compelled to do. It was stupefying, brutalizing work; it left her no time to think, no strength for anything. She was part of the machine she tended, and every faculty that was not needed for the machine was doomed to be crushed out of existence. There was only one mercy about the cruel grind—that it gave her the gift of insensibility. Little by little she sank into a torpor—she fell silent. She would meet Jurgis and Ona in the evening, and the three would walk home together, often without saying a word. Ona, too, was falling into a habit of silence—Ona, who had once gone about singing like a bird. She was sick and miserable, and often she would barely have strength enough to drag herself home. And there they would eat what they had to eat, and afterwards, because there was only their misery to talk of, they would crawl into bed and fall into a stupor, and never stir until it was time to get up again, and dress by candle-light, and go back to the machines. They were so numbed that they did not even suffer much from hunger now; only the children continued to fret when the food ran short.

Yet the soul of Ona was not dead—the souls of none of them were dead, but only sleeping. And now and then they would waken, and these were cruel times. The gates of memory would roll open; old joys would stretch out their arms to them, old hopes and dreams would call to them, and they would stir beneath the burden that lay upon them, and feel its for ever immeasurable weight. They could not even cry out beneath it; but anguish would seize them, more dreadful than the agony of death. It was a thing scarcely to be spoken—a thing never spoken by all the world, that will not know its own defeat.

They were beaten; they had lost the game; they were swept aside. It was not less tragic because it was so sordid, because that it had to do with wages and grocery bills and rents. They had dreamed of freedom; of a chance to look about them and learn something; to be decent and clean; to see their child grow up to be strong. And now it was all gone—it would never be! They had played the game and they had lost. Six years more of toil they had to face before they could expect the least respite, the cessation of the payments upon the house; and how cruelly certain it was that they could never stand six years of such a life as they were living! They were lost, they were going down, and there was no deliverance for them, no hope; for all the help it gave them the vast city in which they lived might have been an ocean waste, a wilderness, a desert, a tomb. So often this mood would come to Ona in the nighttime, when something wakened her. She would lie, afraid of the beating of her own heart, fronting the blood-red eyes of the old primeval terror of life. Once she cried aloud and woke Jurgis, who was tired and cross. After that she learned to weep silently. Their moods so seldom came together now. It was as if their hopes were buried in separate graves.

Jurgis, being a man, had troubles of his own. There was another spectre following him. He had never spoken of it, nor would he allow anyone else to speak of it—he had never acknowledged its existence to himself. Yet the battle with it took all the manhood that he had—and once or twice, alas! a little more. Jurgis had discovered drink.

He was working in the steaming pit of hell, day after day, week after week, until now there was not an organ of his body that did its work without pain, until the sound of ocean breakers echoed in his head day and night, and the buildings swayed and danced before him as he went 'own the street. And from all the unending horror of this there was a respite, a deliverance—he could drink! He could forget the pain, he could slip off the burden; he would see clearly again, he would be master of his brain, of his thoughts, of his will. His dead self would stir in him, and he would find himself laughing and cracking jokes with his companions. He would be a man again, and master of his life.

It was not an easy thing for Jurgis to take more than two or three drinks. With the first drink he could eat a meal, and he could persuade himself that that was economy; with the second he could eat another meal. But there would come a time when he could eat no more, and then to pay for a drink was an unthinkable extravagance, a defiance of the age-long instincts of his hunger-haunted class. One day, however, he took the plunge, and drank up all that he had in his pockets, and went home half 'piped', as the men phrase it. He was happier than he had been in a year; and yet, because he knew that the happiness would not last, he was savage, too—with those who would wreck it, and with the world, and with his life. And then, again, beneath this, he was sick with the shame of himself. Afterward, when he saw the despair of his family, and reckoned up the money he had spent, the tears came into his eyes, and he began the long battle with the spectre.

It was a battle that had no end, that never could have one. But Jurgis did not realize that very clearly; he was not given much time for reflection. He simply knew that he was always fighting. Steeped in misery and despair as he was, merely to walk down the street was to be put upon the rack. There was surely a saloon on the corner—perhaps on all four corners, and some in the middle of the block as well; and each one stretched out a hand to him—each one had a personality of its own, allurements unlike any other. Going and coming—before sunrise and after dark—there was warmth and a glow of light, and the steam of hot food, and perhaps music, or a friendly face, and a word of good cheer. Jurgis developed a fondness for having Ona on his arm whenever he went out on the street, and he would hold her tightly, and walk fast. It was pitiful to have Ona know of this—it drove him wild to think of it; the thing was not fair, for Ona had never tasted drink, and could not understand. Sometimes, in desperate hours, he would find himself wishing that she might learn what it was, so that he need not be ashamed in her presence. They might drink together, and escape from the horror—escape for a while, come what would.

So there came a time when nearly all the conscious life of Jurgis consisted of a struggle with the craving for liquor. He would have ugly moods, when he hated Ona and the whole family, because they stood in his way. He was a fool to have married; he had tied himself down, had made himself a slave. It was all because he was a married man that he was compelled to stay in the yards; if it had not been for that he might have gone off like Jonas, and to hell with the packers. There were few single men in the fertilizer mill—and those few were working only for a chance to escape. Meantime, too, they had something to think about while they worked—they had the memory of the last time they had been drunk, and the hope of the time when they would be drunk again. As for Jurgis, he was expected to bring home every penny; he could not even go with the men at noon-time—he was supposed to sit down and eat his dinner on a pile of fertilizer dust.

This was not always his mood, of course; he still loved his family. But just now was a time of trial. Poor little Antanas, for instance—who had never failed to win him with a smile—little Antanas was not smiling just now, being a mass of fiery red pimples. He had had all the diseases that babies are heir to in quick succession—scarlet fever, mumps, and whooping-cough in the first year, and now he was down with measles. There was no one to attend to him but Kotrina; there was no doctor to help him because they were too poor, and children did not die of the measles—at least, not often. Now and then Kotrina would find time to sob over his woes, but for the greater part of the time he had to be left alone, barricaded upon the bed. The floor was full of draughts, and if he caught cold he would die. At night he was tied down, lest he should kick the covers off him, while the family lay in their stupor of exhaustion. He would lie and scream for hours, almost in convulsions; and then, when he was worn out, he would lie whimpering and wailing in his torment. He was burning up with fever, and his eyes were running sores; in the day-time he was a thing uncanny and impish to behold, a plaster of pimples and sweat, a great purple lump of misery.

Yet all this was not really as cruel as it sounds, for, sick as he was, little Antanas was the least unfortunate member of that family. He was quite able to bear his sufferings—it was as if he had all these complaints to show what a prodigy of health he was. He was the child of his parents' youth and joy; he grew up like the conjuror's rose-bush, and all the world was his oyster. In general, he toddled around the kitchen all day with a lean and hungry look—the portion of the family's allowance that fell to him was not enough, and he was unrestrainable in his demand for more. Antanas was but little over a year old, and already no one but his father could manage him.

It seemed as if he had taken all of his mother's strength—had left nothing for those that might come after him. Ona was with child again now, and it was a dreadful thing to contemplate; even Jurgis, dumb and despairing as he was, could not but understand that yet other agonies were on the way, and shudder at the thought of them.

For Ona was visibly going to pieces. In the first place she was developing a cough, like the one that had killed old Dede Antanas. She had had a trace of it ever since that fatal morning when the greedy streetcar corporation had turned her out into the rain; but now it was beginning to grow serious, and to wake her up at night. Even worse than that was the fearful nervousness from which she suffered; she would have frightful headaches and fits of aimless weeping; and sometimes she would come home at night shuddering and moaning, and would fling herself down upon the bed and burst into tears. Several times she was quite beside herself and hysterical; and then Jurgis would go half mad with fright. Elzbieta would explain to him that it could not be helped, that a woman was subject to such things when she was pregnant; but he was hardly to be persuaded, and would beg and plead to know what had happened. She had never been like this before, he would argue; it was monstrous and unthinkable. It was the life she had to live, the accursed work she had to do, that was killing her by inches. She was not fitted for it—no woman was fitted for it, no woman ought to be allowed to do such work; if the world could not keep them alive any other way it ought to kill them at once and be done with it. They ought not to marry, to have children; no working man ought to marry. If he, Jurgis, had known what a woman was like, he would have had his eyes torn out first. So he would carry on, becoming half hysterical himself, which was an unbearable thing to see in a big man; Ona would pull herself together and fling herself into his arms, begging him to stop, to be still, that she would be better, it would be all right. So she would lie and sob out her grief upon his shoulder, while he gazed at her, as helpless as a wounded animal, the target of unseen enemies.

FIVE SPEECHES

These five famous addresses show the place great oratory holds in the history of the country. Pivotal moments in the life of the republic can be defined or described by a great speech, and each of these five speeches punctuates an era: the War of Independence (a speech given by Patrick Henry, 1736–1799); the Civil War (Abraham Lincoln, 1809–1865); the fight for womens' rights (Susan B. Anthony, 1820–1906); the New Deal (Franklin Delano Roosevelt, 1882–1945); and the nineteen sixties (John F. Kennedy, 1917–63).

GIVE ME LIBERTY, OR GIVE ME DEATH

Patrick Henry

RICHMOND, VA, MARCH, 23, 1775

Mr. President: No man thinks more highly than I do of the patriotism, as well as abilities of the very worthy gentlemen who have just addressed the House. But different men often see the same subject in different lights; and, therefore, I hope that it will not be thought disrespectful to those gentlemen, if, entertaining as I do, opinions of a character very opposite to theirs, I shall speak forth my sentiments freely and without reserve. This is no time for ceremony. The question before the House is one of awful moment to this country. For my own part I consider it as nothing less than a question of freedom or slavery; and in proportion to the magnitude of the subject ought to be the freedom of the debate. It is only in this way that we can hope to arrive at truth, and fulfill the great responsibility which we hold to God and our country. Should I keep back my opinions at such a time, through fear of giving offence, I should consider myself as guilty of treason towards my country, and of an act of disloyalty towards the majesty of heaven, which I revere above all earthly kings.

Mr. President, it is natural to man to indulge in the illusions of hope. We are apt to shut our eyes against a painful truth, and listen to the song of that siren, till she transforms us into beasts. Is this the part of wise men, engaged in a great and arduous struggle for liberty? Are we disposed to be of the number of those who, having eyes, see not, and having ears, hear not, the things which so nearly concern their temporal salvation? For my part, whatever anguish of spirit it may cost, I am willing to know the whole truth; to know the worst and to provide for it.

I have but one lamp by which my feet are guided; and that is the lamp of experience. I know of no way of judging of the future but by the past. And judging by the past, I wish to know what there has been in the conduct of the British ministry for the last ten years, to justify those hopes with which gentlemen have been pleased to solace themselves and the House? Is it that insidious smile with which our petition has been lately received? Trust it not, sir; it will prove a snare to your feet. Suffer not yourselves to be betrayed with a kiss. Ask yourselves how this gracious reception of our petition comports with these warlike preparations which cover our waters and darken our land. Are fleets and armies necessary to a work of love and reconciliation? Have we shown ourselves so unwilling to be reconciled, that force must be called in to win back our love? Let us not deceive ourselves, sir. These are the implements of war and subjugation; the last arguments to which kings resort.

I ask gentlemen, sir, what means this martial array, if its purpose be not to force us to submission? Can gentlemen assign any other possible motives for it? Has Great Britain any enemy, in this quarter of the world, to call for all this accumulation of navies and armies? No, sir, she has none. They are meant for us; they can be meant for no other. They are sent over to bind and rivet upon us those chains which the British ministry have been so long forging. And what have we to oppose to them? Shall we try argument? Sir, we have been trying that for the last ten years. Have we anything new to offer on the subject? Nothing. We have held the subject up in every light of which it is capable; but it has been all in vain. Shall we resort to entreaty and humble supplication? What terms shall we find which have not been already exhausted? Let us not, I beseech you, sir, deceive ourselves longer. Sir, we have done everything that could be done, to avert the storm which is now coming on. We have petitioned; we have remonstrated; we have supplicated; we have prostrated ourselves before the throne, and have implored its interposition to arrest the tyrannical hands of the ministry and Parliament. Our petitions have been slighted; our remonstrances have produced additional violence and insult; our supplications have been disregarded; and we have been spurned, with contempt, from the foot of the throne. In vain, after these things, may we indulge the fond hope of peace and reconciliation. There is no longer any room for hope. If we wish to be free—if we mean to preserve inviolate those inestimable privileges for which we have been so long contending—if we mean not basely to abandon the noble struggle in which we have been so long engaged, and which we have pledged ourselves never to abandon until the glorious object of our contest shall be obtained, we must fight! I repeat it, sir, we must fight! An appeal to arms and to the God of Hosts is all that is left us!

They tell us, sir, that we are weak; unable to cope with so formidable an adversary. But when shall we be stronger? Will it be the next week, or the next year? Will it be when we are totally disarmed, and when a British guard shall be stationed in every house? Shall we gather strength by irresolution and inaction? Shall we acquire the means of effectual resistance, by lying supinely on our backs, and hugging the delusive phantom of hope, until our enemies shall have bound us hand and foot? Sir, we are not weak, if we make proper use of the means which the God of nature hath placed in our power. Three millions of people, armed in the holy cause of liberty, and in such a country as that which we possess, are invincible by any force which our enemy can send against us. Besides, sir, we shall not fight our battles alone. There is a just God who presides over the destinies of nations; and who will raise up friends to fight our battles for us. The battle, sir, is not to the strong alone; it is to the vigilant, the active, the brave. Besides, sir, we have no election. If we were base enough to desire it, it is now too late to retire from the contest. There is no retreat, but in submission and slavery! Our chains are forged! Their clanking may be heard on the plains of Boston! The war is inevitable—and let it come! I repeat it, sir, let it come!

It is in vain, sir, to extenuate the matter. Gentlemen may cry peace, peace—but there is no peace. The war is actually begun! The next gale that sweeps from the north will bring to our ears the clash of resounding arms! Our brethren are already in the field! Why stand we here idle? What is it that gentlemen wish? What would they have? Is life so dear, or peace so sweet, as to be purchased at the price of chains and slavery? Forbid it, Almighty God! I know not what course others may take; but as for me, give me liberty, or give me death!

The Gettysburg Address

Abraham Lincoln

Gettysburg, PA, November 19, 1863

Fourscore and seven years ago our fathers brought forth on this continent a new nation, conceived in liberty and dedicated to the proposition that all men are created equal. Now we are engaged in a great civil war, testing whether that nation, or any nation so conceived and so dedicated, can long endure.

We are met on a great battlefield of that war. We have come to dedicate a portion of that field as a final resting place for those who here gave their lives that that nation might live. It is altogether fitting and proper that we should do this. But, in a larger sense, we cannot dedicate—we cannot consecrate—we cannot hallow—this ground.

The brave men, living and dead, who struggled here have consecrated it far above our poor power to add or to detract. The world will little note nor long remember what we say here, but it can never forget what they did here.

It is for us, the living, rather to be dedicated here to the unfinished work which they who fought here have thus far so nobly advanced. It is rather for us to be here dedicated to the great task remaining before us—that from these honored dead we take increased devotion to that cause for which they gave the last full measure of devotion; that we here highly resolve that these dead shall not have died in vain; that this nation, under God, shall have a new birth of freedom; and that government of the people, by the people, for the people, shall not perish from the earth.

ARE WOMEN PERSONS?

Susan B. Anthony

Friends and fellow-citizens: I stand before you tonight under indictment for the alleged crime of having voted at the last Presidential election, without having a lawful right to vote. It shall be my work this evening to prove to you that in thus voting, I not only committed no crime, but, instead, simply exercised my citizen's rights, guaranteed to me and all United States citizens by the National Constitution, beyond the power of any State to deny.

The preamble of the Federal Constitution says:

"We, the people of the United States, in order to form a more perfect union, establish justice, insure domestic tranquillity, provide for the common defense, promote the general welfare, and secure the blessings of liberty to ourselves and our posterity, do ordain and establish this Constitution for the United States of America."

It was we, the people; not we, the white male citizens; nor yet we, the male citizens; but we, the whole people, who formed the Union. And we formed it, not to give the blessings of liberty, but to secure them; not to the half of ourselves and the half of our posterity, but to the whole people—women as well as men. And it is a downright mockery to talk to women of their enjoyment of the blessings of liberty while they are denied the use of the only means of securing them provided by this democratic-republican government—the ballot.

For any State to make sex a qualification that must ever result in the disfranchisement of one entire half of the people is to pass a bill of attainder, or an *ex post facto* law, and is therefore a violation of the supreme law of the land. By it the blessings of liberty are forever withheld from women and their female posterity. To them this government has no just powers derived from the consent of the governed. To them this government is not a democracy. It is not a republic. It is an odious aristocracy; a hateful oligarchy of sex; the most hateful aristocracy ever established on the face of the globe; an oligarchy of wealth, where the rich govern the poor. An oligarchy of learning, where the educated govern the ignorant, or even an oligarchy of race, where the Saxon rules the African, might be endured; but this oligarchy of sex, which makes father, brothers, husband, sons, the oligarchs over the mother and sisters, the wife and daughters of every household—which ordains all men sovereigns, all women subjects, carries dissension, discord and rebellion into every home of the nation.

Webster, Worcester and Bouvier all define a citizen to be a person in the United States, entitled to vote and hold office.

The only question left to be settled now is: Are women persons? And I hardly believe any of our opponents will have the hardihood to say they are not. Being persons, then, women are citizens; and no State has a right to make any law, or to enforce any old law, that shall abridge their privileges or immunities. Hence, every discrimination against women in the constitutions and laws of the several States is today null and void, precisely as is every one against Negroes.

THE ONLY THING WE HAVE TO FEAR IS FEAR ITSELF

Franklin Delano Roosevelt

WASHINGTON, D.C., MARCH 4, 1933

I am certain that my fellow Americans expect that on my induction into the Presidency I will address them with a candor and a decision which the present situation of our Nation impels. This is preeminently the time to speak the truth, the whole truth, frankly and boldly. Nor need we shrink from honestly facing conditions in our country today. This great Nation will endure as it has endured, will revive and will prosper. So, first of all, let me assert my firm belief that the only thing we have to fear is fear itself—nameless, unreasoning, unjustified terror which paralyzes needed efforts to convert retreat into advance. In every dark hour of our national life a leadership of frankness and vigor has met with that understanding and support of the people themselves which is essential to victory. I am convinced that you will again give that support to leadership in these critical days.

In such a spirit on my part and on yours we face our common difficulties. They concern, thank God, only material things. Values have shrunken to fantastic levels; taxes have risen; our ability to pay has fallen; government of all kinds is faced by serious curtailment of income; the means of exchange are frozen in the currents of trade; the withered leaves of industrial enterprise lie on every side; farmers find no markets for their produce; the savings of many years in thousands of families are gone.

More important, a host of unemployed citizens face the grim problem of existence, and an equally great number toil with little return. Only a foolish optimist can deny the dark realities of the moment.

Yet our distress comes from no failure of substance. We are stricken by no plague of locusts. Compared with the perils which our forefathers conquered because they believed and were not afraid, we have still much to be thankful for. Nature still offers her bounty and human efforts have multiplied it. Plenty is at our doorstep, but a generous use of it languishes in the very sight of the supply. Primarily this is because rulers of the exchange of mankind's goods have failed through their own stubbornness and their own incompetence, have admitted their failure, and have abdicated. Practices of the unscrupulous moneychangers stand indicted in the court of public opinion, rejected by the hearts and minds of men.

True they have tried, but their efforts have been cast in the pattern of an outworn tradition. Faced by failure of credit they have proposed only the lending of more money. Stripped of the lure of profit by which to induce our people to follow their false leadership, they have resorted to exhortations, pleading tearfully for restored confidence. They know only the rules of a generation of self-seekers. They have no vision, and when there is no vision the people perish.

The moneychangers have fled from their high seats in the temple of our civilization. We may now restore that temple to the ancient truths. The measure of the restoration lies in the extent to which we apply social values more noble than mere monetary profit.

Happiness lies not in the mere possession of money; it lies in the joy of achievement, in the thrill of creative effort. The joy and moral stimulation of work no longer must be forgotten in the mad chase of evanescent profits. These dark days will be worth all they cost us if they teach us that our true destiny is not to be ministered unto but to minister to ourselves and to our fellow men.

Recognition of the falsity of material wealth as the standard of success goes hand in hand with the abandonment of the false belief that public office and high political position are to be valued only by the standards of pride of place and personal profit; and there must be an end to a conduct in banking and in business which too often has given to a sacred trust the likeness of callous and selfish wrongdoing. Small wonder that confidence languishes, for it thrives only on honesty, on honor, on the sacredness of obligations, on faithful protection, on unselfish performance; without them it cannot live.

Restoration calls, however, not for changes in ethics alone. This Nation asks for action, and action now.

Our greatest primary task is to put people to work. This is no unsolvable problem if we face it wisely and courageously. It can be accomplished in part by direct recruiting by the Government itself, treating the task as we would treat the emergency of a war, but at the same time, through this employment, accomplishing greatly needed projects to stimulate and reorganize the use of our natural resources.

Hand in hand with this we must frankly recognize the overbalance of population in our industrial centers and, by engaging on a national scale in a redistribution, endeavor to provide a better use of the land for those best fitted for the land. The task can be helped by definite efforts to raise the values of agricultural products and, with this, the power to purchase the output of our cities. It can be helped by preventing realistically the tragedy of the growing loss through foreclosure of our small homes and our farms. It can be helped by insistence that the Federal, State, and local governments act forthwith on the demand that their cost be drastically reduced. It can be helped by the unifying of relief activities which today are often scattered, uneconomical, and unequal. It can be helped by national planning for and supervision of all forms of transportation and of communications and other utilities which have a definitely public character. There are many ways in which it can be helped, but it can never be helped merely by talking about it. We must act and act quickly.

Finally, in our progress toward a resumption of work we require two safeguards against a return of the evils of the old order: there must be a strict supervision of all banking and credits and investments, so that there will be an end to speculation with other people's money; and there must be provisions for an adequate but sound currency.

These are the lines of attack. I shall presently urge upon a new Congress, in special session, detailed measures for their fulfillment, and I shall seek the immediate assistance of the several States.

Through this program of action we address ourselves to putting our own national house in order and making income balance outgo. Our international trade relations, though vastly important, are in point of time and necessity secondary to the establishment of a sound national economy. I favor as a practical policy the putting of first things first. I shall spare no effort to restore world trade by international economic readjustment, but the emergency at home cannot wait on that accomplishment.

The basic thought that guides these specific means of national recovery is not narrowly nationalistic. It is the insistence, as a first consideration, upon the interdependence of the various elements in and parts of the United States—a recognition of the old and permanently important manifestation of the American spirit of the pioneer. It is the way to recovery. It is the immediate way. It is the strongest assurance that the recovery will endure.

In the field of world policy I would dedicate this Nation to the policy of the good neighbor—the neighbor who resolutely respects himself and, because he does so, respects the rights of others—the neighbor who respects his obligations and respects the sanctity of his agreements in and with a world of neighbors.

If I read the temper of our people correctly, we now realize as we have never realized before our interdependence on each other; that we cannot merely take but we must give as well; that if we are to go forward, we must move as a trained and loyal army willing to sacrifice for the good of a common discipline, because without such discipline no progress is made, no leadership becomes effective. We are, I know, ready and willing to submit our lives and property to such discipline, because it makes possible a leadership which aims at a larger good. This I propose to offer, pledging that the larger purposes will bind upon us all as a sacred obligation with a unity of duty hitherto evoked only in time of armed strife.

With this pledge taken, I assume unhesitatingly the leadership of this great army of our people dedicated to a disciplined attack upon our common problems.

Action in this image and to this end is feasible under the form of government which we have inherited from our ancestors. Our Constitution is so simple and practical that it is possible always to meet extraordinary needs by changes in emphasis and arrangements without loss of essential form. That is why our constitutional system has proved itself the most superbly enduring political mechanism the modern world has produced. It has met every stress of vast expansion of territory, of foreign wars, of bitter internal strife, of world relations.

It is to be hoped that the normal balance of Executive and legislative authority may be wholly adequate to meet the unprecedented task before us. But it may be that an unprecedented demand and need for undelayed action may call for temporary departure from that normal balance of public procedure.

I am prepared under my constitutional duty to recommend the measures that a stricken Nation in the midst of a stricken world may require. These measures, or such other measures as the Congress may build out of its experience and wisdom, I shall seek, within my constitutional authority, to bring to speedy adoption.

But in the event that the Congress shall fail to take one of these two courses, and in the event that the national emergency is still critical, I shall not evade the clear course of duty that will then confront me. I shall ask the Congress for the one remaining instrument to meet the crisis—broad Executive power to wage a war against the emergency, as great as the power that would be given to me if we were in fact invaded by a foreign foe.

For the trust reposed in me I will return the courage and the devotion that befit the time. I can do no less.

We face the arduous days that lie before us in the warm courage of national unity; with the clear consciousness of seeking old and precious moral values; with the clear satisfaction that comes from the stern performance of duty by old and young alike. We aim at the assurance of a rounded and permanent national life.

We do not distrust the future of essential democracy. The people of the United States have not failed. In their need they have registered a mandate that they want direct, vigorous action. They have asked for discipline and direction under leadership. They have made me the present instrument of their wishes. In the spirit of the gift I take it.

In this dedication of a Nation we humbly ask the blessing of God. May He protect each and every one of us. May He guide me in the days to come.

ASK NOT WHAT YOUR COUNTRY CAN DO FOR YOU

John F. Kennedy

WASHINGTON, D.C., JANUARY 20, 1961

We observe today not a victory of party but a celebration of freedom—symbolizing an end as well as a beginning—signifying renewal as well as change. For I have sworn before you and Almighty God the same solemn oath our forebears prescribed nearly a century and three quarters ago.

The world is very different now. For man holds in his mortal hands the power to abolish all forms of human poverty and all forms of human life. And yet the same revolutionary beliefs for which our forebears fought are still at issue around the globe—the belief that the rights of man come not from the generosity of the state but from the hand of God.

We dare not forget today that we are the heirs of that first revolution. Let the word go forth from this time and place, to friend and foe alike, that the torch has been passed to a new generation of Americans—born in this century, tempered by war, disciplined by a hard and bitter peace, proud of our ancient heritage—and unwilling to witness or permit the slow undoing of those human rights to which this nation has always been committed, and to which we are committed today at home and around the world.

Let every nation know, whether it wishes us well or ill, that we shall pay any price, bear any burden, meet any hardship, support any friend, oppose any foe to assure the survival and the success of liberty.

This much we pledge—and more.

To those old allies whose cultural and spiritual origins we share, we pledge the loyalty of faithful friends. United, there is little we cannot do in a host of cooperative ventures. Divided, there is little we can do—for we dare not meet a powerful challenge at odds and split asunder.

To those new states whom we welcome to the ranks of the free, we pledge our word that one form of colonial control shall not have passed away merely to be replaced by a far more iron tyranny. We shall not always expect to find them supporting our view. But we shall always hope to find them strongly supporting their own freedom—and to remember that, in the past, those who foolishly sought power by riding the back of the tiger ended up inside.

To those peoples in the huts and villages of half the globe struggling to break the bonds of mass misery, we pledge our best efforts to help them help themselves, for whatever period is required—not because the Communists may be doing it, not because we seek their votes, but because it is right. If a free society cannot help the many who are poor, it cannot save the few who are rich.

To our sister republics south of our border, we offer a special pledge—to convert our good words into good deeds—in a new alliance for progress—to assist free men and free governments in casting off the chains of poverty. But this peaceful revolution of hope cannot become the prey of hostile powers. Let all our neighbors know that we shall join with them to oppose aggression or subversion anywhere in the Americas. And let every other power know that this hemisphere intends to remain the master of its own house.

To that world assembly of sovereign states, the United Nations, our last best hope in an age where the instruments of war have far outpaced the instruments of peace, we renew our pledge of support—to prevent it from becoming merely a forum for invective—to strengthen its shield of the new and the weak—and to enlarge the area in which its writ may run.

Finally, to those nations who would make themselves our adversary, we offer not a pledge but a request: that both sides begin anew the quest for peace, before the dark powers of destruction unleashed by science engulf all humanity in planned or accidental self-destruction.

We dare not tempt them with weakness. For only when our arms are sufficient beyond doubt can we be certain beyond doubt that they will never be employed.

But neither can two great and powerful groups of nations take comfort from our present course—both sides overburdened by the cost of modern weapons, both rightly alarmed by the steady spread of the deadly atom, yet both racing to alter that uncertain balance of terror that stays the hand of mankind's final war.

So let us begin anew—remembering on both sides that civility is not a sign of weakness, and sincerity is always subject to proof. Let us never negotiate out of fear. But let us never fear to negotiate.

Let both sides explore what problems unite us instead of belaboring those problems which divide us.

Let both sides, for the first time, formulate serious and precise proposals for the inspection and control of arms—and bring the absolute power to destroy other nations under the absolute control of all nations.

Let both sides seek to invoke the wonders of science instead of its terrors. Together let us explore the stars, conquer the deserts, eradicate disease, tap the ocean depths and encourage the arts and commerce.

Let both sides unite to heed in all corners of the earth the command of Isaiah—to "undo the heavy burdens ... [and] let the oppressed go free."

And if a beachhead of cooperation may push back the jungles of suspicion, let both sides join in creating a new endeavor—not a new balance of power, but a new world of law, where the strong are just and the weak secure and the peace preserved.

All this will not be finished in the first hundred days. Nor will it be finished in the first thousand days, nor in the life of this Administration, nor even perhaps in our lifetime on this planet. But let us begin.

In your hands, my fellow citizens, more than mine, will rest the final success or failure of our course. Since this country was founded, each generation of Americans has been summoned to give testimony to its national loyalty. The graves of young Americans who answered the call to service surround the globe.

Now the trumpet summons us again—not as a call to bear arms, though arms we need—not as a call to battle, though embattled we are—but a call to bear the burden of a long twilight struggle, year in and year out, "rejoicing in hope, patient in tribulation"—a struggle against the common enemies of man: tyranny, poverty, disease and war itself.

Can we forge against these enemies a grand and global alliance, north and south, east and west, that can assure a more fruitful life for all mankind? Will you join in that historic effort?

In the long history of the world, only a few generations have been granted the role of defending freedom in its hour of maximum danger. I do not shrink from this responsibility—I welcome it. I do not believe that any of us would exchange places with any other people or any other generation. The energy, the faith, the devotion which we bring to this endeavor will light our country and all who serve it—and the glow from that fire can truly light the world.

And so, my fellow Americans: ask not what your country can do for you—ask what you can do for your country.

My fellow citizens of the world: ask not what America will do for you, but what together we can do for the freedom of man.

Finally, whether you are citizens of America or citizens of the world, ask of us here the same high standards of strength and sacrifice which we ask of you. With a good conscience our only sure reward, with history the final judge of our deeds, let us go forth to lead the land we love, asking His blessing and His help, but knowing that here on earth God's work must truly be our own.

ANTHEMS AND
SONGS

The historical antedecents of songs and anthems are often obscure. The legend of Johnny Appleseed, the romantic story of the bountiful stranger helping the hapless pioneer, has long been a popular one. Here it is rendered by William Henry Venable (1836–1920), a writer and long-time teacher in Cincinnati. The song "Yankee Doodle" probably originated in a British tune which was co-opted by the American side in the Revolutionary War. The song became so popular that it was played at the surrender of General Cornwallis at Yorktown in 1781. "Dixie" was written by Daniel Decatur Emmett (1815–1904), who founded the Virginia Minstrels in 1842. The song became the standard of the Confederacy during the Civil War, a counterpart to "John Brown's Body." Katherine Lee Bates (1859–1929), who wrote the text of "America the Beautiful," was a poet and educator. She taught at Wellesley from 1885 to 1925. The poet James Weldon Johnson and his brother John Rosamund Johnson collaborated in 1899 to produce "Lift Every Voice and Sing," a celebration of Lincoln's birthday. The former wrote the words; the latter the music. Francis Scott Key (1779– 1843) is the author of "The Star-Spangled Banner," the national anthem.

Johnny Appleseed

William Henry Venable

A midnight cry appalls the gloom,
    The puncheon door is shaken:
"Awake! arouse! and flee the doom!
    Man, woman, child, awaken!

"Your sky shall glow with fiery beams
    Before the morn breaks ruddy!
The scalpknife in the moonlight gleams,
    Athirst for vengeance bloody!"

Alarumed by the dreadful word
    Some warning tongue thus utters,
The settler's wife, like mother bird,
    About her young ones flutters.

Her first-born, rustling from a soft
    Leaf-couch, the roof close under,
Glides down the ladder from the loft,
    With eyes of dreamy wonder.

The pioneer flings open wide
    The cabin door, naught fearing;
The grim woods drowse on every side,
    Around the lonely clearing.

"Come in! come in! nor like an owl
    Thus hoot your doleful humors;
What fiend possesses you to howl
    Such crazy, coward rumors?"

The herald strode into the room;
    That moment, through the ashes,

The back-log struggled into bloom
   Of gold and crimson flashes.

The glimmer lighted up a face,
   And o'er a figure dartled,
So eerie, of so solemn grace,
   The bluff backwoodsman startled.

The brow was gathered to a frown,
   The eyes were strangely glowing,
And, like a snow-fall drifting down,
   The stormy beard went flowing.

The tattered cloak that round him clung
   Had warred with foulest weather;
Across his shoulders broad were flung
   Brown saddlebags of leather.

One pouch with hoarded seed was packed,
   From Penn-land cider-presses;
The other garnered book and tract
   Within its creased recesses.

A glance disdainful and austere,
   Contemptuous of danger,
Cast he upon the pioneer,
   Then spake the uncouth stranger:

"Heed what the Lord's anointed saith;
   Hear one who would deliver
Your bodies and your souls from death;
   List ye to John the Giver.

"Thou trustful boy, in spirit wise
   Beyond thy father's measure,
Because of thy believing eyes
   I share with thee my treasure.

"Of precious seed this handful take;
  Take next this Bible Holy:
In good soil sow both gifts, for sake
  Of Him, the meek and lowly.

"Farewell! I go!—the forest calls
  My life to ceaseless labors;
Wherever danger's shadow falls
  I fly to save my neighbors.

"I save; I neither curse nor slay;
  I am a voice that crieth
In night and wilderness. Away!
  Whoever doubteth, dieth!"

The prophet vanished in the night,
  Like some fleet ghost belated;
Then, awe-struck, fled with panic fright
  The household, evil-fated.

They hurried on with stumbling feet,
  Foreboding ambuscado;
Bewildered hope told of retreat
  In frontier palisado.

But ere a mile of tangled maze
  Their bleeding hands had broken,
Their home-roof set the dark ablaze,
  Fulfilling doom forespoken.

The savage death-whoop rent the air!
  A howl of rage infernal!
The fugitives were in Thy care,
  Almighty Power eternal!

Unscathed by tomahawk or knife,
  In bosky dingle nested,

The hunted pioneer, with wife
  And babes, hid unmolested.

The lad, when age his locks of gold
  Had changed to silver glory,
Told grandchildren, as I have told,
  This western wildwood story.

Told how the fertile seeds had grown
  To famous trees, and thriven;
And oft the Sacred Book was shown,
  By that weird Pilgrim given.

Remember Johnny Appleseed,
  All ye who love the apple;
He served his kind by Word and Deed,
  In God's grand greenwood chapel.

YANKEE DOODLE

Father and I went down to camp,
   Along with Captain Gooding;
And there we see the men and boys
   As thick as hasty pudding.
Chorus
Yankee Doodle keep it up,
   Yankee Doodle dandy,
Mind the music and the step,
   And with the girls be handy.

And there we see a thousand men,
   As rich as Squire David;
And what they wasted ev'ry day,
   I wish it could be saved.

And there was Captain Washington
   Upon a slapping stallion,
A-giving orders to his men;
   I guess there was a million.

And then the feathers on his hat,
   They looked so very fine, ah!
I wanted peskily to get
   To give to my Jemima.

And there I see a swamping gun,
   Large as a log of maple,
Upon a mighty little cart;
   A load for father's cattle.

And every time they fired it off,
   It took a horn of powder;
It made a noise like father's gun,
   Only a nation louder.

And there I see a little keg,
   Its head all made of leather,
They knocked upon't with little sticks,
   To call the folks together.

And Cap'n Davis had a gun,
   He kind o' clapt his hand on't
And stuck a crooked stabbing-iron
   Upon the little end on't.

The troopers, too, would gallop up
   And fire right in our faces;
It scared me almost half to death
   To see them run such races.

It scared me so I hooked it off,
   Nor stopped, as I remember,
Nor turned about till I got home,
   Locked up in mother's chamber.

Dixie

Daniel Decatur Emmett

I wish I was in de land ob cotton,
Old times dar am not forgotten,
    Look away! Look away! Look away! Dixie Land.
In Dixie Land whar' I was born in,
Early on one frosty mornin',
    Look away! etc.
Chorus
Den I wish I was in Dixie, Hoo-ray! Hoo-ray!
In Dixie Land, I'll take my stand to lib and die in Dixie;
Away, away, away down south in Dixie,
Away, away, away down south in Dixie.

Old Missus marry Will-de-weaber,
Willium was a gay deceaber;
    Look away! etc.
But when he put his arms around 'er
He smiled as fierce as a forty-pounder,
    Look away! etc.

His face was sharp as a butcher's cleaber,
But dat did not seem to greab 'er;
    Look away! etc.
Old Missus acted the foolish part,
And died for a man dat broke her heart,
    Look away! etc.

Now here's a health to the next old Missus,
And all de gals dat want to kiss us;
    Look away! etc.
But if you want to drive 'way sorrow,
Come and hear dis song to-morrow,
    Look away! etc.

Dar's buckwheat cakes an' Injun batter,
Makes you fat or a little fatter;
   Look away! etc.
Den hoe it down and scratch your grabble,
To Dixie's land I'm bound to trabble,
   Look away! etc.

AMERICA THE BEAUTIFUL

Katharine Lee Bates

O beautiful for spacious skies,
    For amber waves of grain,
For purple mountain majesties
    Above the fruited plain!
America! America!
    God shed His grace on thee
And crown thy good with brotherhood
    From sea to shining sea!

O beautiful for pilgrim feet,
    Whose stern, impassioned stress
A thoroughfare for freedom beat
    Across the wilderness!
America! America!
    God mend thine every flaw,
Confirm thy soul in self-control,
    Thy liberty in law!

O beautiful for heroes proved
    In liberating strife,
Who more than self their country loved,
    And mercy more than life!
America! America!
    May God thy gold refine,
Till all success be nobleness
    And every gain divine!

O beautiful for patriot dream
    That sees beyond the years
Thine alabaster cities gleam
    Undimmed by human tears!
America! America!
    God shed His grace on thee,
And crown thy good with brotherhood
    From sea to shining sea!

LIFT EVERY VOICE AND SING

James Weldon Johnson

Lift every voice and sing
Till earth and heaven ring,
Ring with the harmonies of Liberty;
Let our rejoicing rise
High as the listening skies,
Let it resound loud as the rolling sea.
Sing a song full of the faith that the dark past has taught us,
Sing a song full of the hope that the present has brought us.
Facing the rising sun of our new day begun,
Let us march on till victory is won.

Stony the road we trod,
Bitter the chastening rod,
Felt in the days when hope unborn had died;
Yet with a steady beat,
Have not our weary feet
Come to the place for which our fathers sighed?
We have come over a way that with tears has been watered,
We have come, treading our path through the blood of the
     slaughtered,
Out from the gloomy past,
Till now we stand at last
Where the white gleam of our bright star is cast.

God of our weary years,
God of our silent tears,
Thou who hast brought us thus far on the way;
Thou who hast by Thy might
Led us into the light,
Keep us forever in the path, we pray.
Lest our feet stray from the places, our God, where we
     met Thee,

Lest, our hearts drunk with the wine of the world, we
    forget Thee;
Shadowed beneath Thy hand,
May we forever stand.
True to our God,
True to our native land.

THE STAR-SPANGLED BANNER

Francis Scott Key

Oh, say, can you see, by the dawn's early light,
What so proudly we hailed at the twilight's last gleaming,
Whose broad stripes and bright stars through the perilous
    fight,
O'er the ramparts we watched were so gallantly streaming?
And the rockets' red glare, the bombs bursting in air,
Gave proof thro' the night that our flag was still there.
Oh, say, does that star-spangled banner yet wave
O'er the land of the free, and the home of the brave!

On the shore, dimly seen thro' the mists of the deep,
Where the foe's haughty host in dread silence reposes,
What is that which the breeze o'er the towering steep,
As it fitfully blows, half conceals, half discloses?
Now it catches the gleam of the morning's first beam,
In full glory reflected, now shines on the stream.
'Tis the star-spangled banner; oh, long may it wave
O'er the land of the free, and the home of the brave!

And where is that band who so vauntingly swore
That the havoc of war and the battle's confusion
A home and a country should leave us no more?
Their blood has washed out their foul footsteps'
    pollution.
No refuge could save the hireling and slave
From the terror of flight, or the gloom of the grave:
And the star-spangled banner in triumph doth wave
O'er the land of the free, and the home of the brave!

Oh, thus be it ever when freemen shall stand
Between their loved homes and the war's desolation
Blest with victory and peace, may the heaven-rescued
    land

Praise the power that hath made and preserved us a
    nation!
Then conquer we must, when our cause it is just,
And this be our motto: "In God is our trust!"
And the star-spangled banner in triumph doth wave,
O'er the land of the free, and the home of the brave!

A NOTE ON THE TYPE

The principal text of this Modern Library edition
was set in a digitized version of Janson,
a typeface that dates from about 1690 and was cut by Nicholas Kis,
a Hungarian working in Amsterdam. The original matrices have
survived and are held by the Stempel foundry in Germany.
Hermann Zapf redesigned some of the weights and sizes for Stempel,
basing his revisions on the original design.